Advance

She's ba-a-ack! Since the publication of her first book, *What Was It I Was Saying?*, we've been waiting for more pages from Ann Ipock. There's something magical about the way Ann presents everyday events in her life. Believe me, this is just the beginning of dozens of humorous tales...We cheer her on while waiting for her next book.

—NANCY RHYNE, AUTHOR OF
Lowcountry Voices, What the People on the Backroads Told Me About Ghosts, Sea Captains, and Charleston Jazzmen

Wow! What an entertaining book of fun essays. Ann's upbeat, positive outlook on life shows through in all of her personal narratives. Ann has an uncanny ability to take the mundane, everyday things around us, things most of us don't think twice about, and make them interesting and funny. Ann has an extraordinary talent—she can turn anything into a great story.

—DELORES BLOUNT, PUBLISHER OF
STRAND MEDIA GROUP

A sure cure for taking life too seriously is Ann Ipock's latest book, *Life Is Short, But It's Wide.* Ann has the uncanny ability of seeing humor in life's everyday experiences and situations be they mundane or unexpected. You can't help but laugh as you read these anecdotes, and most of the time you remember having experienced something similar. Keep this book of short reads in a handy spot so Ann can help you replace a frown with a smile or a gloomy outlook with a full-bellied guffaw.

—BETH WILLIAMS, EDITOR IN CHIEF OF
Pee Dee Magazine

Life Is Short, But It's Wide reflects Ann Ipock at her most wildly intuitive. She has captured the magical essence of the South Carolina Lowcountry and the heart of the Pawleys Island mystique in this uninhibited volume of wisdom and experience. Within these pages you just might recognize yourself—or find something precious you thought you lost. She is right—wild women don't get the blues.

—ELIZABETH ROBERTSON HUNTSINGER,
AUTHOR OF *Ghosts of Georgetown*

Your book is a testament to your talent and hard work. Each column provides interesting and unique insights into life in the Palmetto State that our citizens will find both comforting and entertaining...

—JIM HODGES, FORMER S.C. GOVERNOR

It's been over five years since I was first introduced to Ann Ipock's writings. A North Carolina transplant to the Lowcountry of South Carolina, Ann's newspaper columns have been compared to humorist Erma Bombeck, *only better*, according to one newspaper pundit. Her reflections of the South are like letters from home, wrapped in sweet-smelling jasmine, and delivered with a smile. She has a knack for making us feel welcome, whether it's in Granny Pinky's kitchen or in her Pawleys Island living room. The South that Ann writes about is neither old nor new. It is part of the past and a piece of the present; it exists as surely as peach orchards, front porches, country roads, and Spanish moss. Her stories are as palatable as grits, boiled peanuts, pileau, and collard greens. Looking at this region through Ann's eyes clarifies what was, and is, going down in Dixie through her personal experiences and observations. Her humor is deeply rooted in the soil of her beloved South, and the words she uses to describe personal situations are as Southern as her drawl. This is Ann Ipock's South. Welcome.

—JESSE TULLOS, EDITOR OF
Georgetown Times

Life Is Short, But It's Wide

(In the Southern State of Reality)

all the best,
Ann Ipock

R2-1

ANN IPOCK

Life Is Short, But It's Wide (In the Southern State of Reality) by Ann Ipock

published by

Carolina Avenue™ PRESS

PO Box 775, 114 Carolina Avenue South, Boonville, NC 27011
e-mail: carolinaavepress@yadtel.net

First edition 2003
Copyright © 2003 by Ann Ipock

Portions of this book have appeared in different form in *Georgetown Times*, *Pee Dee Magazine*, and *Sasee*, and are reprinted with permission.

Applied for Library of Congress Cataloging-in-Publication Data

09 08 07 06 05 04 03   7 6 5 4 3 2 1
ISBN 0-9718231-2-X

To contact the author for speaking engagements:
e-mail: amipock@sc.rr.com
write: Ann Ipock, PO Box 3212, Pawleys Island, SC 29585
Web site: www.annipock.com

Book design and production by Whitline Ink Incorporated
Cover design by K. Scott Whitaker, Whitline Ink Incorporated
Printed in the United States of America

This book is dedicated

with deep love and tremendous gratitude
to my husband, Russell, and daughters,
Katie Ipock and Kelly Ipock Stunda. And
to my parents, Billy and Louise Morris,
whose real-life story is truly a miracle!

Table of Contents

Thanks, and Keep on Reading 1

Chapter 1: Haute Cuisine (aka Cooking My Goose)

The Carolinas' Four Food Groups: Grease, Slime, Sweets, and Brine . . . 7
Supper Club Night on a Budget? Not at $2,942.45! 9
Bon Appetit! 11
Gumbo, Jumbo, What a Big Mumbo! 13
Cooking Out: Trying to Grill Is Not Such a Thrill. 15
GRITS: "Get Ready If They Stick" 17
Living with the Thanksgiving Hex. 19
Chow-Chow Can Cure What Ails You. 21
Losing Your Mind in Aisle Five. 24

Chapter 2: Hobbies and Other Dangerous Diversions

Rosemary Is for Remembrance, and How! 29
Garden Club: The Unlikely Self-Defense Group. 31
Caution: Deep-Digging Wife in Flip-Flops Ahead 33
A Good Thing? Silver Frogs and Trilingual Mosquitoes 35
Where, Oh Where, Is Jim Cantore? 37
Boats and Buckets, No Whales, Oh My!. 39
Ticks and Wedding Potpourri. 42
Acting or Directing—A Double Threat 44
Friends, Gamecock Football, and Amazing Grace 46
America's Health: Too Much of a Good Thing? 49
Shagging After He Left the Farm. 51
This Chick Gets Her Kicks with Greenbax Stamps. 53

Chapter 3: You Talk Funny, Guess You're Not Southern

Those Taters Have Eyes and Other Sassy Southern Sayings. 57
Wild Women Don't Get the Blues. 59
Snip, Snap, or Sniff? 62
Opposites Attract...But Don't Iron 64
Two Heads (But Not Two Names) Are Better than One 66
You Wouldn't Understand, It's a Shopping Thing 68
The Girls' Trip Away (You Go, Girl!) 71
You Made Your Bed, Now Lie (Not Nap) in It 73
My Dad's Gone Psychic 75
Does the Song Say "I'm No Fool" (And How Would I Know)? 78
No, Virginia, There Is No Oat Cheese 80
Real Southern Ladies Don't Use Toothpicks 82
Forty-Something, Foolish, and Free. 84

Chapter 4: General Observations from the Nut House

Hold Your Tongue and Forget the Gum 89
Bathroom Break: It's No Longer Just a Woman Thing 91
Long Live the Romay! 93
Ode to Snoring and Puffing 95
Where Do Broken Hearts Go? Home to Mama! 97
For Whom the Bell Eventually Tolls: The Seven-Hour Wedding 99
Did You Read *The Book?* 102
Pile High! The Importance of Being Ordered 104
Welcome to My Home, and Watch Your Step 106
Secret Service Men...So Cool They Make Me Drool 108
Those Aren't My Shoes! They're Too Clean 111

Chapter 5: Fighting Technology and Other Culprits

I'm Seeing Red, But I'm Not Feeling Blue 115
Voice Mail? Voice Misery? Press, Repeat, and Hold 119
Carrying Forward the Fight Against Mold 121
Colorful Solutions to Purse Snatching 123
You Don't Smell Swell, and You're Giving Me a Headache 125
Cars Versus UOFs (Unidentified Ongoing Fiascos) 127
Car Talk (The Joy of Tune-Ups) 129
Having One of Those Days? 131
A New Set of Eyes 133
The Lizard and the Rug 135
The Day the Alligator's Noose Got Loose 137
The Mayor and the Mustache 139
Body Work for People, Not Cars 141
Where's Spartanburg, and Can You Get There from Here? 143
Big Hair Means the Big Time (Commitment, That Is) 146
Some Folks Lose Things, Some Get Lost 148

Chapter 6: Granny Pinky: The Grande Dame

Pay-Ya Preserves and Fickled Pigs 153
Rat Cheese and Common Courtesy 155
Granny Pinky and the Shoe Stretcher 157
Red Bows and Painted Toes 159
Granny Pinky's Stolen Plymouth and the Fourth of July 160
The Never-Ending Afghan 162
A Hot Stove and a Fast Car 163
A Rich Inheritance, Indeed 165

Acknowledgements 167

Thanks, and
Keep on Reading!

My career as a dental hygienist ended abruptly the day I got the mayor's mustache caught in my tooth polisher. But instead of sitting around wringing my hands, I found a new profession: I picked up my pen and began writing. More oddities happened, and I wrote about them, too.

My family has come to expect the unexpected when I'm around. Russell, my husband, is a church administrator…so he isn't allowed to cuss or get angry with me *ever*. He's such a good sport that he even let me tell about the time he nearly bit his tongue in half and ended up at the ER, thanks to defective chewing gum. Our daughter Kelly is a kindergarten teacher and married to Chuck; they're the parents to our beautiful granddaughter, Madison, age two. Our daughter Katie is a USC-Columbia sophomore, where she is majoring in flute performance. They're all extremely kind and patient to allow me to include them in print on a regular basis.

When I began to document these happenings about careers, family, mishaps, and mayhem, I needed a vehicle for my work. My first published piece ran in *Pee Dee Magazine*, followed by *Georgetown Times*, where I continue to write a biweekly humor column. I also found outlets in *Sasee*, *Strand Magazine*, and *Gateway*, and discovered I can't stop writing (and these oddities won't stop happening)! Soon I had an overflowing pile of columns, which congealed into a first compilation, and here I am watching a second stack of papers transform into that most magical of things known as *a book*.

Frequently I run into readers in the grocery store, on the beach, downtown, in restaurants, at the beauty shop, and at the mall, who remark that some of the things I've mentioned in my columns have happened to them, a friend, or a family member.

For instance, my catching the oven and microwave on fire, enduring life with a golf fanatic, test-driving a red sports car, aging gracefully, living with a snoring spouse, and perfecting the art of Southern cooking. Readers also mention Granny Pinky's stolen car and her well-groomed dog, Mark, quacky business ventures, unwanted critters, the art of womanhood (hair and fingernails are biggies for me), and bad-luck cars.

I'm often told I look familiar. Once a woman stopped me in a bookstore and asked if she knew me. I told her no, I didn't think so. She kept on, not taking no for an answer, with: Where did I work? Where did I live? What was my name? I gave her my life history with every tiny detail (but one). She stood there shaking her head, saying, *No, that's not it,* about ten times. One last try, I thought. I said, *I do write a column for the* Georgetown Times. She nearly gave me a heart attack, jumping up and down, yelling, *That's it! That's it!* I thought I learned something that day: *Whenever people say I look familiar, tell them I'm a writer.* I'd keep the story consistent that way.

I've also had strangers ask if they knew me, only to find out they really didn't. As I said, most times the inquirer turns out to be a reader, but sometimes not. The dialogue below happened recently, right in the parking lot of the Piggly Wiggly in Pawleys Island:

What's your name? You look so familiar.
    Ann Ipock.
    Where do I know you from?
    I don't know. I work at home.
    Are you a public official? A town spokesperson?
    No.
    Let me see, let me see…(scratching her head) *I've seen you somewhere before. Where was it?*
        With smiling anticipation, I said, *I do write a column for the* Georgetown Times.
        She shook her head. *No, that's not it. I don't read the paper.*

Oh well. And if life weren't complicated enough, there is another person who has the same name I have. Ann Ipock. Confusing, but true. See, there was an Ann E. Ipock who lived in Pawleys before I moved here. Years ago, when I lived in Myrtle Beach, we met over the phone and then once in person, when I worked for a telephone company and was her business representative. I've since been told that she moved away, but I still get mistaken for her at the bank, the doctor's office, and the pharmacy. With a last name like Ipock, you wouldn't think there would be two of us, but there are. Let me set the record straight: I am Ann M. Ipock.

Funny things happen to us writers, but one of my pet peeves is when an author has her photograph printed on a book cover or a column and the photo is, say, twenty-five years old. As a matter of fact, I just had an updated photo taken, since I like to practice what I preach. Okay, that, and the fact that a friend once saw a dressy photo of me, taken before glamour shots became popular, but along that line. In this picture, my bare shoulders are draped with a white feather boa, my hair is teased just so, and my makeup puts Mary Kay to shame. Surprised, she asked me who was *that*, followed by, *Are you sure? What happened? You don't look at all like her.*

So, from Ann M. Ipock, who looks exactly like the photograph you see here today on the back of this book, I say, *Thanks, and keep on reading!*

chapter 1

Haute Cuisine
(aka Cooking My Goose)

The Carolinas' Four Food Groups: Grease, Slime, Sweets, and Brine

Welcome to the Carolinas, birthplace of the original four food groups. (So what if the American Dietary Association copied us with their own version a few years later?) Tourist season is fast approaching, and I just wanted to let everyone know what a treat is in store for them.

Here, we've got every meal, snack, social affair, and family gathering covered. First, you'll need to have a notion of exactly what you have a hankering for. In other words, just keep reading until you run across something to your liking.

Our main food group here is grease, otherwise known as fat. Trust me, we've got plenty of it! At the top of the list is fried pork skins—the real thing you get at barbecue joints, not that packaged Styrofoam-looking stuff they sell at grocery stores. Other greasy Southern classics include biscuits, fried chicken, baby back ribs, pulled pork, french fries, onion rings, and my personal favorite, mayonnaise. You can find these foods anywhere in North and South Carolina, but my pick is the greasy diners tucked away "out in the sticks," as we call it. Just ask any local for a recommendation.

Next, and a close second, is the slime category. This includes oysters, raw or steamed, okra, and three-day-old boiled peanuts. We catch and/or grow this tasty trio—my personal favorites—right here in coastal Carolina and have a long line of forefathers who did the very same thing. Spam and Vienna sausage fit into this category nicely. Some Southerners insist mayonnaise does as well (see "grease" above), but I disagree.

Third is sweets. No decent Southerner would be caught dead without them in their home. At the top of the sweets list are store-bought moon pies. We are famous for pound cake (plain, please), lemon meringue pie, and doughnuts. (Residents of my native state, North Carolina, are extra proud of Winston-Salem, home of Krispy Kreme.) And there's the queen of sugar herself, sweet tea. My husband boycotts dining establishments that don't serve sweet tea, being as how it's a Southern tradition.

Last, but not least, is the brine food group. Anything with salt and/or vinegar fits in here. Take pickled pigs' feet, for instance. I wouldn't touch them with a ten-foot pole, but when I was growing up that was my father's favorite Friday night dish. He would close the shoe store at 8:00 p.m., come home and have his own special "cold plate" made up by my mother, complete with saltine crackers, boiled eggs, and hunks of rat cheese. We Southerners can pickle just about anything. I myself have "put up" pickled figs. We also pickle squash, string beans, and eggs. When we pickle watermelon rind, we add cinnamon and red food dye. (Don't ask me why.) Pickled peaches, pears, and apple rings are popular, too.

So, there you have it: Grease, slime, sweets, and brine. Maybe eventually we'll add a fifth group for vegetables. After all, we are big on collards, rutabaga, and turnip greens. Nah, then someone might say we're showing off, just trying to copy the American Dietary Association.

Supper Club Night on a Budget? Not at $2,942.45!

We're in a wonderful supper club. Nine couples, all living in Myrtle Beach (except us, in Pawleys Island), get together every two months and enjoy stimulating conversation, relaxation, and entertainment, all the while catching up on everyone's lives. I might mention we have some fabulous storytellers in this group. We also feast upon the most exquisite meals.

Another reason it's so wonderful is that I only have to host the event every two years or so. Thankfully, my turn just passed. I had put it off as long as I possibly could, citing every reason known to humankind. I told them I misplaced my kitchen dishes (all but one, Jean Hussey, believed it). I told them we had a hurricane that only hit the tip of Pawleys Island, but Clay Brittain, III, figured that one out. I told them I didn't know how to cook, but Kay Nicholson said they already knew that. I told them that we'd moved to Atlanta, but Peggy Sansbury and Sherry Smith drove by my house and saw me planting flowers later that day. Normally, it's not so terribly expensive to host supper club. The host provides the entrée and calls the other couples, who each sign up for one of the other categories: appetizer, starch, vegetable, salad, dessert, etc. Simple, so far. Then the real fun begins, at least for me. I get to play Martha Stewart.

Picture this: freshly cut flowers, ironed tablecloths and matching linens, polished silver, squeaky clean crystal. If you really want to impress guests, you can buy new kitchen towels. This time, I went a little crazy and bought bathroom "velvet towels" as my husband, Russell, calls them, that don't soak up an ounce of water. In fact, when you step out of the shower and dry off, you end up with even more water on your body. Can't figure that out! Also, they shed and leave behind those little bitty lint balls that end up all over your house, all over your body, and even threaten a fire in the dryer vent. Even with all these purchases, you can still normally budget the big event with an expenditure of oh, fifty dollars or less.

But not Ann. Oh, no, I have to be different. To *not* be different is just so boring, and boredom is paramount to "coma-dom" to me. Imagine the shocked look on Russell's face when I told him that this particular soirée set us back about $2,942.45. Let me clarify.

The main culprit was the berber carpet we bought for our four-bedroom home right before the club met. We were long overdue to replace the worn, soiled, sandy, ratty twelve-year-old carpet. How many people lived here before us I don't know, but it's for sure they had a few pets, dirty paws and all. As for the sand, well, okay. I'll take some responsibility for the beach erosion down here in Pawleys since I track lots of the gritty stuff home after my daily beach walks.

Now, I've already told y'all about my new living room window treatments and two dozen or so pillows. It's true (I confess) that there's no place to sit on the sofa now, but whaddya want? Home fashion or home comfort? Anyway, not one person in the whole supper club complained about standing for hours, though I spotted a few shifting their weight from time to time and saw some leaning up against the wall. In my defense, their feet must have felt pretty darn good with that well-padded carpet beneath their little toes.

Just to prove I'm not a thoughtless person, I will share that I searched out a straight-back chair for guest (and club founder) Beth Ervin, who'd had back surgery a few months ago. (Beth, I'm sorry I couldn't give you a pillow to sit on. They were all lined up perfectly on the sofa and it would have messed up the look.)

The crowning glory in this whole makeover was the cranberry-red foyer that Russell painted and painted and painted. I eventually applied a sponge finish to the wall because the man from Litchfield Hardware said, "Ma'am, you'll never be able to cover the wall with less than seven gallons of paint." I hate it when I'm wrong, so I gave it a shot. I managed to cover it with a single gallon.

You'll recall that my elegant golden-baked crusty flounder with tomatoes, potatoes, and shallots turned out to be, well, flounder mush (read the next story to learn more). No one complained. Heck, I guess it was because they were finally sitting down and it felt so good, they didn't even notice my puréed fish dish.

Bon Appetit!

Russell and I recently hosted a supper club party at which the main entrée, baked flounder, turned out to be mushy flounder. After all those years of reading *Bon Appetit, Southern Living, Veranda*, and *Southern Accents*—not to mention collecting matching dishes, flatware, crystal, serving pieces, unique candles, and beautiful linens, plus acquiring tables and chairs for a big crowd, that night was showtime, buddy! We even had a photographer from *Pee Dee Magazine* shooting pictures of the soiree. We were all dressed in our finest garb, and my new carpet, new window treatments, new pillows, and new foyer were downright stunning.

Everything started out fine. Russell even got in on the action and lined our sidewalk and driveway with attractive luminaries. Our house was sparkling-shiny clean, and I was truly proud. Guest after guest arrived bringing their favorite dishes, carefully prepared and festively arranged. Each dish was perfectly placed on the buffet table which was draped in a colorful tablecloth. The fine spread included roasted asparagus with tri-color peppers, crunchy slaw, candied yams in orange shells, red rice, cornbread, and, of course, seafood. For dessert, we had pumpkin butter, ginger snaps, and key lime pie.

By tradition, the host provides the entrée, and I had picked seafood for the occasion. I decided to have shrimp and flounder—basic staples here on the coast of South Carolina and two of my favorite dishes in the whole world. Old family recipes came to mind, and because I knew two special ones by heart from cooking them umpteen times, I didn't even need a recipe to go by. Really, how could I go wrong with my mother's recipe for spicy buttered shrimp (yum) and Granny Pinky's famous baked flounder?

You know the saying, "Expect the unexpected"? Well, with eighteen hungry guests and one harried chef, it was true that anything could happen. You see, when I ordered the flounder, I inadvertently requested flounder fillet (small and tender, but the key word here is *small*), instead of the whole, meaty fish I'd always cooked before.

11

It was too late to come up with a new recipe, so I just stuck with the old one and hoped for the best. I carefully placed the fillets on the bottom of the pan and added quartered Yukon gold potatoes, canned tomatoes, and shallots. Then I laid bacon strips on top of the flounder. I couldn't cut a slit to hold the bacon inside as I usually did, as the fish was too thin. Still, so far, so good. Next I threw in handfuls of bay leaves. I sprinkled liberal amounts of fresh thyme, basil, and garlic salt, and finished it off with fresh-squeezed lime. I moved the baking pan to the oven shelf and checked on it forty-five minutes later. Uh oh. Crunchy—no, make that hard—potatoes.

Another forty-five minutes later, after opening the oven door a jillion times, I discovered the potatoes were still crunchy. But by then, the flounder had disappeared. Gone! About thirty percent of the original fish remained at the bottom, but it was mush. I guess the other seventy percent evaporated. So, the main entree turned out to be buttered shrimp and fish mush.

The funny part at this point was getting the dish to be photographic (dare I say photogenic?). I managed to throw a few shrimp on top and bring forth whatever fish snippets remained. I forced a smile. Thanks to the side dishes our guests brought, at least I can say with certainty that the meal (minus the flounder) was superb.

After dinner and the mouth-watering desserts, we gathered in the living room and chatted. I did give in and move the two dozen plush pillows from the sofa so we could have an uncrowded place to sit. However, our normal hour of post-meal storytelling didn't last long, maybe because the meal had been served so late and the guests wanted to get home. Too bad. Other nights we've discussed everything from husbands' ratty underwear to wives' Wonderbras, from a wrecker towing a car out of the ocean to snoring husbands and puffing wives. But who could blame this crowd for leaving early? They had stood for hours, been photographed every which-a-way, been forced to eat fish mush, and were just plain old tired.

Oh, well. Everything ended on a cheerful note. We were well-fed, full of bread, and lots was said. Here's a toast to my friends and others out there who gather for fine food and fellowship. Take it from me: It can feed the soul as well as the body. *Bon Appetit!*

Gumbo, Jumbo,
What a Big Mumbo!

I was recently interviewed by Becky Billingsley, features reporter for the Myrtle Beach *Sun-News*. The subject of cooking without a recipe came up, and I told her, sure, I did that all the time. I went on to say my latest experiment was gumbo, and I was still working on getting it right. A few weeks later, I gave up on originality, gave in to tradition, and gave a recipe a shot. The best-sounding gumbo recipe came from *Dairy Hollow House Soup and Bread* by Crescent Dragonwagon, who also writes great children's books. Well. Let's just say it's probably the only time I will ever make gumbo using this recipe. Later, in an e-mail to Becky describing the arduous process, it dawned on me that maybe you'd like to hear what happened.

First, I read over the recipe a couple of times because it was a bit complicated. I reminded myself I was a pro: an experienced cook, a food warrior, a well-seasoned pot-stirrer who had surely tackled bigger jobs than this one. As it turned out, I was sorta, kinda wrong.

The author starts out by quoting Mike Trimble of the *Arkansas Times*: "Youx, Toux, Can Doux a Roux." For those of you who have never heard of a roux, this cookbook defines it as a "highly-seasoned, very thick, vegetarian concentrate, which serves as the stepping-off point for an infinite variety of gumbos."* I spent the greater part of a morning grocery shopping. This Creole delicacy called for twenty-seven ingredients, and the bill totaled fifty dollars. I went home and re-read the recipe. The next morning I got up early to begin the production. For the record, seven hours later, I had achieved a gumbo base. The entire day was spent measuring, washing, chopping, dicing, slicing, stirring, mixing, sweating, cussing, pouting, and moaning.

The recipe required four major steps and making the roux was the first one. I should have realized my short attention span would evaporate after the initial forty-five minutes I spent stirring a cup of flour with a cup of oil. Continuously. "Don't turn away from the stove or the roux will burn," the recipe read (sounding like Cinderella's wicked stepsister). And I didn't turn away. I didn't answer the phone. I didn't turn on the TV. After three cups of coffee, I didn't... Well, you get the picture. I didn't move from that exact spot for forty-five minutes. Chopping and dicing vegetables took a couple more hours. I threw the necessary ingredients into the food processor and pulsed the tomato/spice/herb *mirepoix*, or vegetable sauté. Next, I cooked the mixture in a saucepan and added chicken broth.

When I blended the roux and the *mirepoix*, I ended up with a soup base. I anxiously tasted the gastronomical wonder I'd created. I think it was good. I'm not sure. I was too exhausted and numb for anything to register. Sliding into my easy chair, I began nodding off, but my nap was interrupted when I remembered the kitchen had to be cleaned up. Ack! You've never seen so many pots, pans, skillets, bowls, knives, measuring spoons, and silverware outside of Martha Stewart's housewares collection. I felt like opening the back door and throwing everything out, from dishes to pans to the gumbo itself. (Russell would have applauded this; he hates to wash dishes.)

The nightmare doesn't end there. Why? Because the recipe made what looked like several gallons of gumbo, so the next day I had to buy a few dozen freezer containers. Then wash them. Then fill them.

I'll never do that again. I'll continue to enjoy my cookbooks. Matter of fact, I just joined a cookbook club and have two new selections to read: *Hot, Sour, Salty, Sweet* by Alford and Duguid and *Barefoot Contessa Parties* by Ina Garten. I placed these selections next to my old standbys, *Joy of Cooking* by Rombauer and Becker and *Better Homes and Gardens New Cookbook*. I'll also continue to subscribe to *Bon Appetit* and *Southern Living*. But the next time I mention cooking gumbo, fly me to Louisiana for the real thing. It'd be a lot quicker, and I'm sure a lot more economical.

---

* Cresent Dragonwagon, *Dairy Hollow House Soup & Bread—A Country Inn Cookbook* (New York, NY: Workman Publishing, 1992), p. 236.

Cooking Out: Trying to Grill Is Not Such a Thrill

Has anyone heard if we are having a charcoal shortage? As in charcoal for grilling, light up the fire, and throw on the dogs and burgers. Or, if it's been a really successful grocery store (as we Southerners say) or supermarket (as Northerners say) trip, throw on the steaks! Russell cooked on the grill recently, and he had a little baby mound of charcoal about six-by-six inches piled up. Of course, that was the same night I decided to cook thick, juicy steaks along with grilled veggie and onion packets. As soon as I saw the measly charcoal pile, I started whining, "That's not enough embers." And, naturally, when Russell saw the wide array of food to grill, he began groaning. Thank goodness for microwaves.

Grilling out is supposed to be one of the great American pastimes, but we can't seem to perfect it in our family. We alternate replacing gas grills with charcoal, then go back to gas grills when one of the charcoal grills dies. If you ask me, gas grills always produce a flavorless meal. Sure, the food cooks in no time flat, and the grill lights every time (well, not really, but that's another story). The old-fashioned charcoal method isn't a whole lot better. We buy the ready-to-light charcoal that's supposedly "no starter needed." That's because it's been soaked in gallons of lighter fluid beforehand. Only problem with that is, the food tastes just like kerosene. I mean, let's face it, you can marinate that chicken forever and a day in barbeque, fruit sauce, teriyaki, or whatever, but it always turns out the same.

Last time we had a family cookout, the crowd was sitting there enjoying each other's company, wolfing down great big old burgers, when I stopped chewing and inquired, "Is this the way a burger is supposed to taste?" Everyone added an item or two—another pickle and a slice of onion, maybe a dab of mustard—but nothing disguised the chemical flavor. It sure makes a Jenn-Aire stove sound more and more appealing.

I found out recently I'm not the only person who has grilling nightmares. It seems that two of my friends, Austin and Sel, hosted a pig-pickin' at the annual Carolina-Clemson football game. Sel arrived early at the stadium and made the usual preparations, just as he'd done more times than he could count, firing up the gas grill and placing the pig on the rack. He became suspicious when after about three hours, the temperature gauge pegged out at 500 degrees. When he raised the hood, to his astonishment, the pig was gone. Seems it had been cremated, leaving nothing but ashes and a couple of hard bones.

Sel called Austin to announce the startling news, and they both had a good laugh. Plotting a new course of action, Austin drove to the store to buy a dozen Boston butts to cook. But before putting the roasts on the rack, he "stole" a couple of charred pig bones. For Christmas, he presented Sel with a bright Clemson-orange frame with two black, hard nuggets inside and the following inscription: "Clemson 27–USC 20. November 23, 2002. On this holy day, the chicken was fried and the hog was offered as a burnt sacrifice." (The "chicken" being the USC mascot, the gamecock.)

Stories like this make me yearn for the good old days, don't you agree? That was when the corner Esso station was within a close enough distance to ride your bike, and they sold the usual fare of modern-day grocery stores, as well as gas for your car (and gas prices were fair). Russell's father owned one such store in eastern North Carolina. In fact, his father was a self-taught butcher who specialized in premium-quality meat, freshly cut to order. You could ride your bike over, buy your steak, come home, and your mom or dad would light the grill the old-fashioned way, with charcoal, lighter fluid, and matches. I'd say cooking out was truly a big thrill back then...

GRITS:
"Get Ready If They Stick"

Grits. We Southerners love them. We spend entire evenings dressed up in our finest clothes at dinner parties discussing their merits: color, consistency, brands, what to season them with, what to serve them with, which restaurants serve the best ones. It's kind of an obsession with us corn lovers. After all, that's what grits are—stone-milled corn. Go ahead and add them to other Southern corn dishes we love, like fresh, homegrown corn on the cob, hominy, stewed corn, cornbread, corn dodgers, corn pudding, and polenta.

Though grits taste wonderful, they also have a scary side that few people know about. I've recently had two experiences that prove they can be dangerous. Let me begin by saying, there are a couple of things you should not do with or to grits: cook them in a pot with a mismatched lid and pour dry grits down your garbage disposal.

A couple of years ago, I met five women from Georgia: Rose, Pat, Margaret, Mary Mildred, and Julia Ann. Recently they came back to South Carolina for a visit, and we decided to get together. When I arrived at Julia Ann's cottage, I could tell they had something on their minds. Sure enough, Rose said they'd had a strange experience: They'd cooked grits for breakfast, but couldn't eat them.

"How come?" I asked. Rose went into the kitchen and emerged with a baffled expression on her face and a heavy, aluminum pot full of grits. This was not just any pot, mind you, but one with a mismatched lid that was as good as cemented on. They had tried running the pot and lid under hot water, whacking them with a hammer, prying the lid loose with a screwdriver, and dropping them from the balcony. Nothing worked. The grits were stuck! (A night in the freezer released the tenacious lid the following day.)

The second horror story happened to me. I was cleaning out a cabinet in my kitchen and found a container full of wormy grits. Now don't fuss at me. I'm sorry if this story gets to the squeamish among you. I really am a good housekeeper overall, though checking my pantry for larvae isn't something I do as regularly as say, dusting and vacuuming. Y'all must know that flour, grits, spices, and beans can get icky bugs for whatever reasons…high humidity, old age, non-sealed container. No problem, I thought at the time. I just dumped about ten cups of dry grits into my garbage disposal, added water, and turned it on.

Whish! The design was beautiful. Bright yellow dots of grits swirled among clear water. I even had sound effects—an occasional hiccup followed by a burp. Things were going well until the disposal whined, then groaned to a slow, moaning stop. The water backed up. The grits turned into cement. I took an old long-handled ladle and scooped and scooped, but I couldn't seem to make much progress. The grits actually seemed to multiply. I would scoop, then hit the switch. Nothing. Scoop and hit the switch. Nothing, again.

Finally, Russell came home from work. Oh, how I hated to admit what had happened. I knew he'd tell all my friends and embarrass me. I mean, think about it. I might as well have thrown a bucket of sand down the disposal. "What in the world were you thinking?" Russell asked. The final outcome involved two days of scooping, turning on the disposal, and repeating it all over again. The worst part was (I really hate to tell you this), Russell ended up plunging the sink. Don't worry, I scrubbed it all clean, and it was none the worse for wear. I probably saved myself a hefty plumbing bill, and even more embarrassment in the process.

Let this be a lesson to you. Although grits are a simple food in general, they have a complex side to them. They can destroy heavy cookware and maim unsuspecting garbage disposals, given half a chance. So, I say: Never leave your grits unattended. And to think, that popular slogan reports that "grits" stands for "Girls Raised in the South." My rendition is "Get Ready If They Stick."

Living with the Thanksgiving Hex

You'd think my family would've learned by now that turkeys and I just don't get along. I'm not referring to Russell—y'all lighten up! It's the Thanksgiving holiday that ruffles my feathers, cooks my goose, and gets my goat. It's a disaster each year. And yet my sister Nancy just called from Raleigh and invited her family for the upcoming holiday. She asked, "Do you have plans for Thanksgiving?" to which I replied, "You mean life-threatening or just in general?"

I have had many encounters at Thanksgiving, but here is what comes to mind in recent years. The first Thanksgiving catastrophe is now referred to as "The Martha Stewart Holiday That Wasn't." I don't know, maybe I turned the oven knob a tad bit high (500 degrees is what she suggested). Or could it have been those three yards of oil-soaked cheesecloth wrapped around the turkey? Then again, it might have been the undersized pan. The fourteen-pound turkey hung over the sides, dripping grease onto the bottom of the oven.

In my defense, the number of guests kept growing, and I didn't have time to go to the store to buy a bigger pan. I honestly do not know what caused the explosion. What I do know is that Nancy stood next to the stove and screamed, "Fire!" about the time that I had the potatoes whipped and the celery stuffed—and everybody ran the other way.

Being the quick learner that I am, the following year we Ipocks (with no guests—gee, I wonder why?) went to a nearby restaurant. We were four locals among five hundred tourists, but we all grazed like happy little porkers at an all-you-can-choke-on buffet trough. Before we left, though, our daughter Kelly began to moan, saying she didn't feel so good. At home an hour later, our nineteen-year-old was a commode-hugging, ghostly pale, shaking, trauma victim. As I recall, she slept off the horror for the following twenty-four hours.

The next year, feeling stronger and wiser, I planned to celebrate

Thanksgiving in a way that would've made our forefathers proud. I blocked out the memory of the previous holiday fire and gastrointestinal disaster. We pilgrims were going to have Cornish hens. I reasoned that they were hardly any trouble. I mean, what could go wrong? I'd throw in a few veggies and starches and add some biscuits and desserts. It'd be just wonderful, I promised.

Ha! Everything *was* perfect, to an extent. The table was set with fine china, crystal, and linens fit for a queen, and colorful, aromatic food was displayed just so. Did I mention that I'd arranged fresh flowers? I grabbed my camera. We sat, said grace, then yelled in unison as we carved into the half-cooked poultry oozing bloody juices.

The following year we ventured back to a restaurant and experienced another buffet blunder. Here's the good news: no meal to plan, no dishes to cook, no pots and pans to scrub. Here's the bad news: one waiter, no seats, mostly-empty chafing dishes with only a few morsels of cold, dry food that we scraped off the bottom, and pitiful scraps of turkey, shriveled and hard around the edges. We left the place, heads hung low, dejected, and yes, still hungry!

The fifth experience found us at home once more. Not to be foiled again, we bought a fancy-dancy smoker. We read the directions thoroughly, even quizzed each other afterwards. We were in control and we dared anyone to say otherwise.

We paid particular attention to soaking the hickory chips, lest the bird be flavorless. Russell watched that baby like a hawk. Half a day later, with determined and upbeat attitudes, we sat down to the feast. Everything was delicious except for the turkey, which had the flavor of—you guessed it—a hickory tree.

Russell calls this phenomenon, which seems to have struck only our family, the Thanksgiving Hex. We'll see what happens this year as sixteen hungry holiday celebrants converge at our house. Russell mentioned golf—the guys are happy. I mentioned shopping—the girls are happy. The cousins mentioned the beach—they're happy. My parents mentioned Carolina Opry—we're all happy.

Maybe we'll all be so happy (and busy) that we'll simply forget about the turkey dinner. Just the thought makes me giddy! Hey, does anyone know if Domino's Pizza delivers on Thanksgiving?

Chow-Chow
Can Cure What Ails You

You know the song from *Porgy and Bess* that proclaims something about, "Summertime, and the living is easy"? Well, I would like to add to that, "Produce stands are here, don't you know?" For me, here on the Southern coast, summer officially begins when produce stands open and ends when they close.

Produce stands are about the neatest things we have going for us here in the South, if you ask me. I've purchased some of the best corn on the cob I've ever eaten at a lean-to held up by a couple of two-by-fours, with rickety produce baskets stacked high and an old torn cigar box used for changing money. The people who work at the stands are the *pièce de résistance*. And getting to know them is half the fun.

In my teenage years summering at Bear Creek, North Carolina, my best friend, Jane Summerlin, and I used to lie out on the dock in front of our cottage all day long, listening to beach music on the radio. We would put on our bathing suits, set up our chairs just so, slather on baby oil and iodine from head to toe, and bake our bodies. At lunchtime, we'd race up the hill, push the creaky screen door and run through, and land barefoot in the kitchen to fix ourselves our classic meal: a Bear Creek sandwich, a handful of Fritos, and a cold Coke. Those Bear Creek sandwiches are still my favorite here in Pawleys—ham, cheese, lettuce, fresh home-grown tomatoes, and mayo, piled high on plain white bread (*light* bread, my parents call it). There's nothing better than a home-grown tomato sandwich on that good old light bread. The tomato sandwich must have lots of mayonnaise, salt, and pepper—and don't let it sit too long, or it'll get mushy.

In those big old gardens at Bear Creek, we grew zucchini, eggplant, cucumbers, bell pepper, yellow squash, green beans, corn, new potatoes, cantaloupe, and cabbage, hauling water the first few weeks if we missed getting rain. Every summer Mom would put up bread-and-butter pickles, string beans, tomatoes, pickled watermelon rind (a cinnamon-flavored crunchy treat), and chow-chow, my family's favorite. It's what Northerners call a condiment and Southerners call good eatin'! The finished product is a thing of beauty: a pint jar packed with tiny, glistening chips of green, red, and gold. In my house, it gives coleslaw the twang I crave. Heck, Mom has become famous for her chow-chow in parts of South Carolina these last few years. And I know, because I've delivered many a jar, most notably to my buddies at the produce stands.

One time I took a jar of chow-chow to a dear friend and produce owner in Myrtle Beach. He and his daughter operated the stand, and whenever I stopped to talk to them, I could always count on a smile, a piece of good advice, or just to catch up on the local news and weather. Because I bought many of the ingredients for chow-chow (cabbage, bell pepper, and onion) from this particular stand, I wanted the owner to see for himself how good the finished dish really was. The day I arrived, I noticed he wasn't moving too fast and had a grimace on his face. He was rubbing his lower back with one hand. I handed him the chow-chow and asked what was wrong. He replied, "Awwww, I was in a wreck the other day on the bypass."

"Omigosh," I said. "Are you okay?"

"Yeah. Some guy hit me," he grumbled.

"I am so sorry. Were you wearing your seatbelt?"

He took a step backwards, raised his baseball cap, and dabbed his sweaty brow with a handkerchief. Then he turned to me and said something I'll never forget: "Ya don't wear a seatbelt when yer drivin' a tractor."

We talked a little longer, and I wished him a speedy recovery. Pointing to the jar and its yummy contents, I winked, saying, "Sorry I don't have any chicken soup to offer, but I promise this will cure what ails you."

And you know what? I saw him the next week and he said he was feeling a mite bit better. He also said he sure enjoyed eating that chow-chow with a bowl of navy beans and a piece of cornbread.

Maybe it was just my imagination, but I thought I saw a bounce in his step that I'd never seen before. I guess my mother's chow-chow does have special curative powers, but don't let this get around. She'd be canning 'til the twelfth of never and still wouldn't have enough to feed everybody.

Losing Your Mind
in Aisle Five

There is something about the grocery store that I love. Most of my friends cannot believe it when I tell them I enjoy buying groceries, but it's true. I get a feeling of unleashed power from making a list, loading the buggy as I trek down the aisles, and then going through the checkout. If I have coupons, I'm absolutely euphoric! At the register, they smile and ask you, "Would you like paper or plastic?" as if you're really special. I feel like queen-for-a-day on those trips. I don't know why. Maybe because it's one place I can spend money and not feel guilty. It's hard to justify buying a twelve-dollar bottle of nail polish, but a twelve-dollar Smithfield ham is easy.

My younger daughter, Katie, on the other hand, hates to go to the grocery store. When she was four years old, we would play this game: I had to tell her how many items I was buying, and then she would decide whether to go with me or stay home with her dad. It didn't matter if I said three items and they were spread out all over the store, or ten items in one aisle. She just wanted the number, and the lower the better. In fact, she would not go with me if the number of items was too high. If Katie did go, she counted each article as I placed it in the cart. When I went over the promised number, I had to sneak things in.

My older daughter, Kelly, and my two sisters, Cathy and Nancy, also love to go grocery shopping. Whenever we visit each other, it's usually the first thing we do. Here at the Grand Strand, as we call it, we have lots of other thrilling venues where we can spend our time —such as the beach, golf courses, theaters, nightclubs, amusement parks, and entertainment/shopping meccas—but we have to get the grocery trip out of the way before we head off to do anything else.

When my mother recently came for a visit, as soon as she had unpacked and settled in, off we went to Harris Teeter. They have the same grocery store chain in her town, and her local store was remodeled a couple of years ago. She wanted to compare them, she told me. Mom was once part of a focus group at the Harris Teeter in her hometown. She and a panel of customers would meet each month to evaluate the store, offer suggestions, and commend the programs and ideas that were working well. I suppose old habits are hard to break, and she still has a keen marketing sense.

We strolled into our store in Pawleys that day and she said, "Uh huh. Same as ours—you have your produce on the right when you first walk in." People were watching her with great wonder. Mom picked up a tomato and continued, "Same tomatoes, too." Why is it that we buy these winter, pink-green tomatoes when we know they taste like cardboard? Are we so stuck to our habits—"a salad's not a salad without tomatoes"—that we abandon common sense?

I've had other strange experiences in Harris Teeter, such as the time my friend Nona momentarily lost touch with reality. It began when I saw her lingering at the canned fruit section. It was close to a holiday, so I figured she was making ambrosia. We chatted for a moment while she proceeded to talk about the long hours she was putting in at work, her children's grades at school, and the house-guest she was expecting for the weekend.

After a couple of minutes, I excused myself and headed for the bread counter. Then I realized that, as I sometimes do, I'd forgotten something back in produce. Walking down the long aisle parallel to the meat section, I spotted Nona again—in the same spot. A few minutes later I had to backtrack once more, and poor Nona hadn't moved. She had been standing there all that time, staring at the mandarin oranges, the apricots, and those cutesy pickled peaches.

I walked up to her and patted her on the shoulder. "Nona, honey, it's time to go." In a trance, she took my arm as I guided her back toward the front of the store. I stayed with her as she paid for her can of fruit cocktail, then watched her mosey on to her van, with her teenage children waiting inside—one asleep, one plugged into a Walkman, and the other clearly aggravated.

I always knew someone would have a breakdown in the grocery store, but I figured it would be me...searching for those miniature marshmallows (where are they anyway?) or some other obscure item that I'm convinced the grocer delights in hiding.

Nona's delirium turned out to be temporary. In fact, I saw her the other day. She was giving out samples in front of Harris Teeter. "Delicious fruit mixture with currants, ma'am. Would you like a sample? Here's a fifty-cent coupon." She caught a glimpse of me out of the corner of her eye, looked over, and winked. "If you can't beat 'em, join 'em," she declared.

chapter 2

Hobbies and Other Dangerous Diversions

Rosemary Is for Remembrance, and How!

How many of you folks out there have an herb garden? I did until about a week ago, but the one-hundred-degree rainless days have left only sticks, stakes, and stubbles, and the plants are mostly unrecognizable.

Since rosemary is for remembrance, I remembered after two seasons to quit buying it. That stuff is bad luck in my backyard. On two different occasions, I've had a rosemary plant become dry, turn light brown, and within days, wither to a miniature burnt-looking Christmas tree. Speaking of Christmas, the first winter the plant thrived, and I placed a sprig in everyone's Christmas card. My friend Kay Nicholson says she still keeps her sprig to this day...now if I could just remember where she said she put it.

Once I visited a historic landmark, The Heyward-Washington House, in Charleston, South Carolina. The docent gave us a tour of the home, followed by a tour of the formal gardens. We tourists were delighted with the herb garden, which boasted fragrant lemon balm, pungent tarragon, purple sage, creeping thyme, and feathery dill. The woodsy rosemary, one of my favorite cooking herbs, especially caught my eye. I'd rather grow rosemary at home instead of purchasing it in a grocery store. For me, the appeal of growing rosemary is its year-round availability, lovely scent, and beauty in floral arrangements.

No matter how hard I try, my rosemary never looks like the rosemary in professionally-landscaped gardens. As I mentioned, I'd had two rosemary plants die that year. Seeing the herb garden's healthy specimen, I felt a glimmer of hope. Plus, the docent told us that George Washington had walked along the very path that we were strolling. I don't know for sure, but I'd like to believe the same rosemary plant existed during our nation's first president's visit to Charleston. I thought, *What the heck. If this bush has thrived for two hundred years in Charleston, it ought to make it for one season in Pawleys Island.* I bent over to pinch the plant for an aromatic sniff, and a branch broke off in my hand. What was I to do? I dropped it in my pocket and decided to take it home to see if it would grow. When I got back to my house, I removed the rosemary from my pocket and plunked it in a glass of water. It died within twenty-four hours.

My friend Diane DeVaughn Stokes, host of the television show "Southern Style," recently told me her own rosemary saga. A friend gave her a huge rosemary plant (also grown in Charleston) to transplant to her home in Myrtle Beach. She took a shovel, dug up the plant and surrounding dirt, roots, and pine straw, and placed the rosemary plant in a pot. When she got home, she dug a nice, large hole, lifted the entire dirt ball, and placed it in the ground. Diane watered it and eagerly waited for the plant to grow. At first, everything seemed to be going well. To her delight, she noticed another set of leaves beside the original rosemary plant and thought that it might be basil. This was an added plus, as her friend hadn't mentioned anything about a second herb. Two days later, Diane broke out in a mad itch. After two doctors' visits, it was confirmed that she had a bad case of poison ivy. Armed with gloves and a shovel, Diane had no choice but to dig up the good with the bad, roots and all, and dump the whole mess in a wooded area behind her house.

I'm not sure, but I think the two of us might ought to stick to public speaking and writing. Now whenever I hear someone say, "Rosemary is for remembrance," I add, "And how!" There's no way I could forget the gardening disasters that plagued Diane and me.

Garden Club: The Unlikely Self-Defense Group

Have you ever noticed that the flowers and shrubbery that are the best to decorate with—for Christmas (holly), a wedding shower (smilax), a charity fundraiser (pyracantha)—are the prickly ones? Just ask Russell. I am married to a Paul Bunyan-type who loves to chop down bushes, hack at limbs, and pull up flowers, such as my Oriental poppies, by mistake. "It looked just like a weed," he always mutters as I stand there, disgusted.

Anyway, here is one big ongoing disagreement that Russell and I have. I simply love vines, thorny bushes (roses, especially), and all creeping, climbing plants. He hates them with a passion for various reasons—one being the pain they inflict, be it cuts, scrapes, or rashes. In addition, he likes to remind me that vines such as wisteria can "take over the yard."

I agree it's a tough job trying to cut back gnarly, tangled vines. Even if you think you've killed the plant, new sprouts pop up the next spring. Russell likes basic centipede grass and as little extra greenery as possible. It's easier to mow, he insists.

Russell just doesn't have very good luck with the great outdoors. One evening, our supper club met at Randall Squires' farmhouse in Conway. Six or seven silly men and their daredevil wives (all but me) were showing off. The group climbed a huge old water oak to get a better view of the entire farm—or so they said. I think they did it to prove they still had their youth (though not brains) intact.

Russell was halfway up there, calling to me, "Come on, Ann." I stood firm, shaking my head. I have a strict policy that ladies don't climb trees or hunt animals. Suddenly he slipped and fell, pulling back his thumbnail against the tree bark. I've never seen a burly, ruddy-faced man turn chalky-white so fast. Not only that, he was so weak he was staggering. Heck, I almost had to carry him back to the house. Randall and his wife, Cindy, are both doctors; however, neither specializes in thumbs. They had him soak the wound and apply some antibacterial ointment. The whole experience sure took his appetite away.

I thought Russell had learned his lesson: Mother Nature can be a tough foe to reckon with. I was wrong. A couple of years later, he got into a fight with my prize pyracantha bush when he was cutting it back, and guess who won! He limped into the house holding his thumb and trying to squeeze out the one-inch thorn that was sticking into his bleeding skin. A doctor's visit and ninety-five dollars later, the infection left him feeling sick all week.

Well, it's only October, but I'm already planning my Christmas decorations and arrangements. Russell isn't even getting nervous about the prickly greenery. Why should he? I'm the one who's going to gather, wash, and arrange the dangerous cut branches, just like I do every Christmas season. This is because I love working with live vegetation. Maybe it's a holdover from all those years of being in a garden club, but I've never met a pyracantha, a Japanese barberry, or a thorny rose I didn't like...or have a healthy respect for. Hey, maybe gardening safety is another reason why real ladies wear gloves.

Caution: Deep-Digging Wife in Flip-Flops Ahead

Ever since I was a young adult, I've planted flower beds for beauty and cutting. I have always wanted a cutting garden next to my front door, filled with purple, red, yellow, and magenta flowers, and at least one fresh herb for fragrance. This would be a special area designated "For Ann's Flowers Only," a quiet, sweet spot all my own to enjoy at the end of the day. Finally, I got around to designing my dream garden. The first step was going shopping for some flowers. The next would be digging a bed.

I came home loaded down with a dozen perennials and proceeded to get the shovel out of the garage. Russell watched me with anxiety. I was able to get him out there in the first place because I told him I wanted an opinion. This was true—I wanted an opinion of how much he was willing to help me with this major gardening maneuver, but hey, I'm a little more subtle than that.

No wife in her right mind ever just blurts out, "Hey, honey, can you help me?" because that's a sure ticket to watch your man run the other way, making up some silly excuse, like: "Oops, I just remembered I got a phone call from the repair shop saying the ball bearings I ordered for my lawn mower have come in. In fact, they arrived on an overnight flight from Yugoslavia, and another customer wanted them, and not only that, they are no longer being made, so I better get on down there before they close in five minutes. Bye!"

My dear husband did eventually agree to give me his opinion on where to plant this and that, did the colors complement each other, and did he think it was a sunny enough spot? (As if he would know any of that.) Then I began explaining the real reason I had drug him outside in the ninety-degree heat. Russell folded his arms across his chest. He knew what was coming. When I hinted that I'd like some help digging up the centipede grass, he immediately set the record straight (with an evil crooked smile), saying that he wasn't lifting a finger. "Fine," I said with my jaw set. Who was asking him to?

Anyway, I changed into flip-flops and proceeded to tackle the job on my own. You know what? It was impossible for me to remove that tangled patch of thick, green, healthy centipede with roots as strong as fishing line. For some reason, I could only get a real handle on the job when I dug at a ninety-degree angle, making holes that were about eighteen inches deep. The funny thing was, the deeper I dug, the more powerful I felt. Sure, it left a small gully in my yard, but no problem: I planned to go out the next day and buy around $275 worth of potting soil to fill in the holes.

Russell cringed when he saw I meant business. "Do you have to dig that far down?" he whined. He can't stand it when I dig up good centipede. It's right up there with my selling his golf clubs at a garage sale when he isn't watching.

Finally he succumbed. "Here, let me help you." "Oh no, you're not lifting a finger, remember?" I snapped. Still he stood there, "guarding" the spread of greenery that he was losing mound by mound. Well. After a solid hour of digging up only five square feet by myself, I couldn't stand it any longer. I also couldn't stand up, my back hurt so much. Out of pity (dare I think love?) Russell accepted the shovel and the job was finished in no time flat. As he drove off to get his ball bearings, I hollered, "Look at it this way. One positive thing came out of this, honey. Now you'll have less grass to mow!"

A Good Thing? Silver Frogs and Trilingual Mosquitoes

Is it just me or have we all gone a little "critter crazy" lately? I can remember a time not too long ago when a woman (one of my friends, anyway) would have screamed bloody murder if a frog ever jumped on her blouse. Nowadays, not only do some women have a frog on their blouse, but the darned frog is sterling silver, and pinned down tight. And I know, because I own that beautiful pin, which a dear friend gave me as a birthday gift.

Bug jewelry is a trendy, high-fashion, million-dollar industry. The last time I walked through my favorite boutique in Pawleys I spied gold dragonflies, multicolored beetles, red ladybugs, grasshoppers, and an assortment of fly or spider-looking objects. And it doesn't stop there. Now there are sweaters with weird little creatures emblazoned on them. I talked to a woman the other day who had no fewer than twelve species of critters all over her hand-knitted, $300 sweater, and she smiled when she recited each genus and origin. Never mind that the same woman nearly fainted ten minutes later when she stepped out on the low-country porch of the shop and a lizard scooted across her foot.

Well, I know if I'm ever going to make it in this world, or at least in this part of the country, I just have to get used to the bugs. Heck, did you know some people call the Grand Strand the bug capital of the world? Not really, but they could if they wanted to. You've got your no-see-ums (but you most certainly do-feel-ums), your palmetto bugs, your mosquitoes, your Mayflies, your Japanese beetles, your wasps and dirt dobbers, and in October (the worst of the batch), the yellow jackets. I hear it's a state law that you're not allowed to put on a picnic without 'em.

One time when I was planning a company function at a well-known resort in Myrtle Beach, I shrieked, "Omigosh! Look at that spider," as I watched the woolly insect climb across the seat of the golf cart in which we were taking our outdoor tour. The lady driver, however, didn't understand me. (I won't tell you what part of the country she was from, but let's just say she was Southern-deficient.) She asked me to repeat myself and then said indignantly, "I'm sorry, but I don't know what a *spotter* is."

The worst swarm of bugs I've ever witnessed was in Portsmouth Island, North Carolina, where they have a biennial reunion called "Homecoming." The mosquitoes there were so menacing and blood-thirsty that they could keep up with a boat going forty miles per hour. They were immune to industrial-strength bug spray. And they could speak three different languages—at least, that's what it sounded like when several dozen swarmed my head.

Yes, I'd say bugs and critters are here to stay, be they live creatures or hip jewelry. Isn't it strange how these pests annoy the devil out of us in their natural surroundings, but stick the suckers on a lapel and we're suddenly prancing around saying, "Look at me! Aren't I something with my trendy ladybug pin?" Speaking of trends, maybe a line of accessories will soon follow. Say, for instance, beehive earrings, a spider-web locket, or a lily-pad watch. Better yet, how about a diamond-encrusted flyswatter brooch? Oops, shame on me. Did I say flyswatter? Must have been a Freudian slip.

Where, Oh Where, Is Jim Cantore?

Time is running out, and I'm losing hope of finding that hunky TV announcer Jim Cantore of the Weather Channel on the beach here in Pawleys Island. Since hurricane season officially ends in two weeks, I may as well give it up, huh?

Being an avid reader and writer, I subscribe to three newspapers and a half-dozen magazines, spend quite a lot of time in libraries and bookstores, and have six unread books on my nightstand—not to mention the three I'm currently reading.

I'm not much of a TV watcher. In fact, I rarely turn it on. (The exceptions are "Southern Style," a local cultural events program, some PBS, and a little HGTV.) During hurricane season, though, I do have a favorite station. It's (come on now, guess!), yes, the Weather Channel. Is this because of Dr. Steve Lyons, the surfer boy, or John Hope, the hairdo king? Nope. It's because of that handsome Jim Cantore. I know what some of you are thinking: Is it Jim's darn good looks, his gorgeous tan, his sexy lilting voice, or his biceps? Yes to all four questions. I'm sorry, but when I tune in to Jim, I forget there's a hurricane brewing. I get hypnotized by his charm and then I'm unable to think, much less prepare to evacuate.

During Hurricane Floyd—and who ever named it Floyd anyway? Aren't we getting a little too folksy for major storms? Hurricane Bubba, another countrified choice, will probably be on the list for next year. Anyway, during Floyd, a good friend of mine, Rita, rented a beachfront cottage and invited me over for a birthday luncheon. Off I trekked for a grand tour of the place and a look at the churning water. I knew Floyd was lurking out there *somewhere*, but since the evacuation hadn't been ordered yet, I went out and walked on the beach. I must admit my imagination got a little stirred up (maybe it was the barometric pressure) and I walked for forty-five minutes, searching high and low for Jim. Other beachgoers were looking for shells or watching the waves swell. Not me. I practiced my lines just in case I bumped into Jim and the Weather Channel team. I mean, he's landed at Wrightsville Beach, the Outer Banks, and Wilmington —why not Pawleys Island? I would tell him all about my recently published book and how the viewers could order it. Never mind that he would be interviewing me about the hurricane. I'd figured out a way of working in my sales pitch.

This is what I had rehearsed: "Yes, Jim, Governor Hodges [a fine man who has read my first book, I might add!] is indeed about to announce whether there will be a mandatory evacuation, and yes, Jim, I'll be leaving if the Governor says we must. However, I have a deadline with the *Georgetown Times* for my weekly column entitled 'What Was It I Was Saying?' I'm hoping the storm goes out to sea. Anyway, what better time than now to settle in with a good read?" Phew! Alas, I came home, turned on the boob tube and there he was—Jim, that is—in Wrightsville Beach. I had two choices: Stand there and watch that good-looking hunk until the lights went out or drive to Wrightsville Beach looking for him. I stayed home, glued to the TV set.

And to our current South Carolina leader, Governor Sanford: The next time we're faced with an approaching hurricane, please try to persuade the Weather Channel to send Jim Cantore down here for pre-storm coverage. Maybe I'd get to meet Jim in person and he could interview me. Then I'd gladly follow orders to evacuate.

Hey, do you think that Jim would give me a lift on his way out of town?

Boats and Buckets, No Whales, Oh My!

Well folks, I've "gone and done it," as the Shania Twain song says. Whale watching, that is. Make that, I attempted whale watching, along with eighty-eight or so other nervous whale-watcher wannabees who braved the thirty-degree, rainy weather and choppy seas in Virginia Beach this past winter.

My best friend Debbie is the Internet travel queen. That's what I call her, anyway. She can always find terrific vacations that boast the best room rates, the most beautiful views, and the greatest adventures —all for a price you won't believe. I didn't believe it at first. Debbie convinced me.

The package she described piqued my interest: A swanky motel room right on the ocean for two nights, a sumptuous lunch valued at seventeen dollars at the premiere hot-hot restaurant in Virginia Beach, admission to the Virginia Museum of Science, and a movie theater ticket—and that was just the beginning. The best part was a chartered boat that would take you out in the Chesapeake Bay, where you could watch whales. Sounded like fun. I told her sure, go ahead and book it.

Now, I subscribe to the theory that you never really get to know a person until you travel overnight with them, and then you often know WTMI, or "way too much information," as my daughter Katie says. We left for Virginia bright and early on a Friday. About twenty miles down the road, Debbie told me she frequently pulls into rest stops. This was already exactly the opposite of road trips with my husband, Russell. We pull over once every, oh, four to ten hours, or thereabouts. This is because I'm busy reading in the car and Russell is hurrying to get to our destination. I really didn't mind the frequent bathroom breaks on our way to Virginia, because even though it was an eight-hour trip, we weren't in any hurry.

An odd thing happened at the first rest stop. It should've been a warning, now that I think back. The automatic toilet flushers and faucets worked just fine for me, but not for Debbie. She explained that she would stand real close to the sensor, move back, stand real close again…but the toilet would not flush. Not only that, but the water from the faucet would not come out. I witnessed the latter. Watching her throw her hands under the faucet over and over was a hoot in itself. I told her she must be missing some neurons or something. Heck, I secretly wondered if she was a space alien. This same scenario played out again at the next rest stop. Honest. I was beginning to feel a little uncomfortable, and you can believe I kept an eye on her while she drove the rest of the trip, just to make sure she didn't vanish into thin air.

We arrived at our motel exhausted but excited. After an initial mix-up in which we got a room with only one double bed, then were moved to a smoking room, we finally settled into our comfortable, oceanfront suite.

After a cozy dinner, we headed back to our room and relaxed. We read, watched TV, chatted, and then crashed. The next day, we awoke to dreary cold skies and headed out for breakfast. The wait-ress gave us her opinion on the whale-watching trip. "It'll be can-celled, I'm sure," she said. She told us the boats never go out when the weather is bad. Hmphhhh, I thought, secretly glad to hear this news. Debbie phoned the marina and was told, oh no, *the ship doth sail*, come rain, wind, or cold. (We had all three.)

One saving grace: Because I don't own any polar-bear gear, I had borrowed Russell's long-handled underwear and his thick, woolly socks. Well, wouldn't you know? I forgot to put on the long johns, but I remembered the socks. Never mind that the heel cup hit my calves. That was probably the best thing I did for myself the entire trip: keep my feet warm.

Y'all, it wasn't fifteen minutes into the trip that the lady beside me got sick. And to think, I wondered why that hundred-gallon trash can (with no lid) was perched in the middle of the boat. *These people are going to eat a bunch of nabs and drink a lot of Pepsis*, I thought. Not exactly.

I felt waves of queasiness come and go. Thirty minutes passed before the unmistakable nausea grabbed hold of me. I nonchalantly told Debbie (who now had numb biceps, as I'd been holding on to them for dear life) that I didn't feel well. Trouper that she is, she lurched forward, grabbed the trash can, and placed it under my chin. Up came the eggs Benedict I'd had for breakfast. Let me tell you: There is sick and then there is *really* sick. I never wanted to see land so bad in my life.

Right after that, the tour guide meandered through, presenting his lecture on whales. Was it my imagination, or did he wink at me? His voice (and face, for that matter) faded in and out. I could not concentrate. I sat there with a fixed stare. Finally I just said, "Blugh-hhhhhh" as I once again lost it. (You know what I mean.) After I'd dry-heaved four more times, he snarled at me, "I'm sorry I bored you." Was he kidding?

Now I'll address the two questions you all must be dying to ask me. No, Debbie did not get sick (and she is still with us to this day, neurons or not). And, no, we did not see any whales. Sad but true. After all, whales are the reason I was out there, feeling perfectly miserable. Otherwise, I would have been home, nice and cozy right here in Pawleys, walking on the beach where it's safe and predictable, picking up shells. No rocking boat. No freezing rain. No array of sickies. No oppressive, heated cabin that made you sweat and shiver at the same time. And, more to the point: no whales. Thank you anyway, but I'm sure I'll enjoy watching the dolphins when they come here in October, as I stand on the beach, my feet firmly planted on solid ground.

Ticks and Wedding Potpourri

I have always loved flowers. Ever since childhood, when I planted a packet of morning glory seeds in the backyard of our home in eastern North Carolina and watched them grow to maturity, I've been hooked.

Over the years, I have had vegetable gardens, flower gardens, and herb gardens. I've had plenty other uses for my gardens as well. I love making tomato sandwiches from freshly-picked tomatoes or spicing a dish with homegrown basil. But my favorite thing to do is dry flowers picked from my yard, as well as wildflowers, and make decorative arrangements, wreaths, and hats.

Russell and Katie are my best supporters (although sometimes reluctantly, I'm sure). Once when we were driving in the mountains, I spotted a field of wildflowers and begged Russell to stop the car. After much bribing and cajoling, he pulled over and I proceeded to cut from the most beautiful field of Queen Anne's lace I had ever seen. I was sitting in the front seat, already planning my next craft project, when I screamed, "Pull over!" My arms were going in one direction and my legs in another, trying to get away from the ticks all over the front seat. I threw out the flowers and expected Russell to throw me out, but he didn't.

Too bad about the Queen Anne's lace because it works well in potpourri, which I've made for several years now. Cathy, my sister in Virginia, creates lovely bowls of richly-smelling flowers, pods, and seeds, and we often compare our mixtures. She uses essential oils, and I confess I never have, although I plan to visit the health food store and see what they offer.

I currently have three containers of my homemade potpourri, and each one has a story behind it. One is from Kelly's wedding; I saved flowers from the table arrangements and bridesmaid's bouquets. The second bunch is from a friend's farm, and includes whole camellias and magnolia pods. The third batch of potpourri includes some dried roses that Russell gave me for my birthday, as well as a few herbs from my home garden. Of these three, my favorite is the wedding potpourri.

When Kelly got married I wanted to add to the wedding in a meaningful yet tasteful and decorative way. I wanted to add my own personal touch. So I decided to make up sachets of potpourri from flowers I had grown that year.

I gathered rose petals, black-eyed Susans, lavender leaves and flowers, lemon verbena, and yarrow. My sister Nancy was staying at a condominium near the beach. She asked me to come over there and we'd make up the bags together.

The lemon verbena wasn't quite dried out, so I placed the whole mixture in the microwave and set it on high for one minute. Then we all heard a bang! The microwave had caught on fire. The verbena was smoldering. The fire went out all by itself, though, and I only had to throw out a spoonful.

I heard the sachets were a big hit at the reception. I saved one back, and it's a good thing, because none was left. Flammable or not, it was my prettiest flower endeavor thus far.

Acting or Directing—
A Double Threat

Well, I've added two more "been there, done that" categories to my resume: wedding direction and community theatre. If you didn't get a chance to see the Murrells Inlet Community Theatre production of "Steel Magnolias," let me tell you, you missed a great play! And no, it had nothing to do with the fact, that I, Ann M. Ipock, portrayed Truvy Jones. Okay, it's true: It was me 100% and then some. The role featured the best of my persona. Where else could I brag on my femininity, get my hair highlighted even blonder, and listen to (and repeat) gossip innocently? Where else could I sashay around wearing a sparkly gold top, rhinestone-studded acrylic heels, and tight blue jeans, and get away with it? Where else could I bond with five other women and come to know their lives inside out, not to mention everyone's brand of underwear (dressing rooms are close quarters)? Where else could I own a beauty shop where I teased and curled hair ("So, we're going to sweep it up but leave some softness around your ears?"), swapped recipes ("Are these chocolate chips semi-sweet or milk?"), and picked out the greatest nail color ("Perfect Passion is my favorite")?

Wedding direction was a little less dramatic, but also had its moments. All I can say to those of you whose wedding I directed is, *Yes, you are legally married.* Actually, recording the covenant was the minister's responsibility, not mine. That's a good thing, because it was tough enough rounding up attendants and having them proceed down the aisle in an orderly fashion, much less hunting down the bride and groom for signatures and witnesses. Reflecting back on those hectic days two years ago when our daughter Kelly got married, I should have known to steer clear of the MOB (Mother of the Bride). All the mothers I worked with were fabulous, but some mysterious tensions mount between the MOB and the bride the week before the wedding.

The day our daughter Kelly got married, she was dressing at the church when she realized her crinoline was nowhere to be found. The kicker was that not one but both of us had carefully checked (and rechecked) to make sure we had every item needed before we left home, twenty-five miles from the church. After she realized the garment was missing, we both remembered the crinoline was stored in our hall coat closet—the one we never used. (Kelly had tried to warn me earlier not to put it there, but I told her, "Honey, it's the only place that monster will fit." I mean, the thing was the size of a small island and it smothered anything nearby.) With tears in her eyes, she said, "Mom, I told you not to put the crinoline in that closet." What was I supposed to do? Carry it around in my arms for four months before the big day? Luckily, a bridesmaid's mother came to the rescue when she ran home and returned with a similar mammoth petticoat.

The funniest thing that happened during a wedding I directed involved the FOB (Father of the Bride). Now, the key word here is "directed." I took my job very seriously. You might say I was directing my own little drama, encouraging the bridal party (otherwise known as the cast) to remember their lines.

During the rehearsal, I explained to the FOB that when the minister said, "Who gives this woman in marriage?" he should be prepared to answer. "For example, you could say, 'Her mother and I do.' Or, 'I do.'" He seemed okay with this.

The next day, I sat in the back pew as usual. The wedding went along without a hitch…until the minister asked, "Who gives this woman in marriage?" You know what the FOB said? "Her mother and I do. Or, I do." Now, you be the judge: Should I stick to acting or directing?

Friends, Gamecock Football, and Amazing Grace

I've recently come to the conclusion that in life it's not necessarily who you know nor what you know, sometimes it's where you go. Take, for instance, my recent visit to First Federal Bank, where I'd only planned to make a deposit. Wrong! Sure, I made the deposit, but I left with an unexpected gift—a sporty new T-shirt displaying the USC Gamecocks. It seems Ellen, my friend and bank teller, had read the *Georgetown Times* column I wrote entitled "Gamecock Football, You Gotta Love It. Or Do You?"

In the column, I told my readers that I had attended my first-ever college football game. It was a near-disaster that resulted in a backache from the serrated metal bleachers, a headache from shouting fans, irritability from an expensive parking fee, fatigue from our mile-long walk in drizzling rain to reach the stadium, sensory overload from a crazy rooster in a black box who turned out to be the Gamecock mascot, and frazzled nerves from watching all those athletes fight over a silly ball. Sports is not my thing. The highlight of the event was watching our daughter Katie, a freshman, play piccolo in the marching band.

At the ballgame, Gamecock T-shirts are projected from a cannon to hopeful spectators. Sadly, I wasn't able to catch one. Ellen must have felt sorry for me. I don't know how she saw me pulling up to the drive-through, but I rounded the corner of the brick building in my SUV and there she stood, gift in hand. I thanked her, promising to wear it right away.

Not only did I get a T-shirt, Austin Beard, the branch manager, emerged from the bank and invited me to a Clemson football game. He was wearing an orange-striped, buttoned-down oxford shirt with a tiger paw embroidered on the pocket. This man was a serious fan! Austin explained the difference between a Clemson football game and a Carolina game. Apparently at Clemson I wouldn't have to deal with smog, exhausting heat, concrete bleachers, and obnoxious outbursts. Since he'd invited me to a game, I asked him if I could pick which one. He shook his head no. I'm no fool—nervy me went right ahead and requested the Carolina-Clemson game anyway. That wasn't possible, he said. Tickets had been sold out to the Clemson-Carolina game (his correction) years ago.

I asked Austin if he had been wearing the aforementioned shirt ever since my column ran a week ago. He reassured me he had not. I asked Ellen if she'd been standing there holding the T-shirt all week. She reassured me she had not. At any rate, the Carolina-Clemson game is being played in less than a week and it doesn't look like I'll be attending.

I did, however, get the chance to attend a second USC game a week after the bank incident. I can't wait to tell Austin. This time I found out there are football games and then there are football games. Let me explain: A dear friend named Willa Wrenn invited Russell and me. She had three tickets for seats on the thirty-five yard line. We'd be sitting with the coachs' wives, holding an invitation to the half-time party. In addition, we had passes to our very own private, red-carpeted bathroom. Willa told us not to worry about bringing our collapsible stadium seats, as we'd be quite comfortable in the individual molded rubber ones in the reserved section. Heck, we had to go through a glass door to get there. We even had our own special parking place and only had to walk about 200 yards to the gate. All this pampering had me singing, "Nothing could be finer than to be in Carolina during football season..." Was it just me, or did the fans surrounding us appear more dignified, the players seem more in control, and even the noise level sound somewhat muted compared to the first USC game we'd gone to?

Before we got to our seats, we toured a Cockaboose. These are individual railroad cars that Carolina fans purchase and convert into plush mini-homes, hosting fabulous tailgating parties the day of the game. Willa's friends were kind enough to invite us inside their Cockaboose where they offered us pizza, chicken, and dessert. I was so comfortable there that I told Willa and Russell to go on to the game and I'd catch up, but they wouldn't.

An even bigger treat awaited us when the game ended. Since we'd left the first game a little early we missed something important—and no, it wasn't the final score. On this night when the clock ran out and the fans began to leave, an eerie silence fell upon the stadium.

Willa said, "Follow me." She took us down to the bleachers, where the marching band was gathered. The musicians stood and played "Amazing Grace," and reverent fans stood silently, transfixed, until the song was over. Then the real cheering began when parents hugged their children who had been playing in the band and well-wishers stepped up to pat the musicians on the back.

I'm afraid I have gotten suckered into that whole team rivalry thing—something I swore I'd never do. So, Austin, I have two things to ask you: Did you notice my "USC Mom" sticker when I left the bank's drive-through the day we chatted? That's what I am now, and I'm wearing the T-shirt to prove it. However, we can still be friends. Oh, and if a ticket does show up for the Carolina-Clemson game, would you have your people contact my people?

America's Health: Too Much of a Good Thing?

We Americans are an often fascinating, always changing, and sometimes contradictory bunch. Keeping abreast of the tremendous flow of information health experts dish out, for instance, requires focus and attention. I consider myself to be as informed, open-minded, and progressive as any woman I know. I mean, hey, I'm all for holistic health. Alternative medicine is a subject I enjoy researching. I believe the mind, body, and spirit have an undeniable connection and that attitude shapes us all. And yes, I agree that eating garlic daily will make you live longer. (No one can stand to get near you, so you never catch any germs!)

Being a medical transcriptionist, I'm aware of the importance of proper back care and exercise. So imagine my surprise when, out of the blue, I started having persistent backaches. I investigated and found some startling facts about heavy shoulder bags and strained vertebrae, which I'd like to share with the women of America.

It seems the Pocketbook Manufacturers' Association and the National Chiropractic Association have gotten together to pad their purses, so to speak. Suitcase-sized, heavy pocketbooks will and do cause us damage in the way of unequal shoulder heights, discombobulated spines, and cervical spasms. Just ask anyone who's trying to find her checkbook in the checkout line while feeding her wailing baby a kiddie cup of juice and answering her cell phone, which is buried at the bottom of the weighted object slung over her shoulder.

It might not be a bad idea for chiropractors and orthopedic surgeons to install a set of special scales in their offices just to weigh our purses. I can hear it now. "Ms. Ipock, seeing as how your pocketbook weighs more than you do, you might want to consider one for each shoulder to be balanced." Then they'd send me into a room where it just so happened they had matching Gucci leather bags.

I've wised up to this conspiracy. Every two or three days, I rid my purse of those eight leaking pens, name badge with the pin that jams underneath my fingernail, and loose coins (usually pennies— no wonder there's a shortage). I even bought a teensy, tiny Barbie-doll purse, but it was so small my checkbook stuck out of it.

I have also noticed a health hazard involving tourists who lug around massive articles on their stays here. When I'm walking on the beach, I often catch a glimpse of a family moving into a summer rental. After forking out a thousand dollars or more to rent a cottage, you'd think they'd take it easy for a few days: slathering oil on their bodies, sweating, tanning, and reading.

First, however, they must check in, which means spending hours trudging up flights of stairs with suitcases, hang-up bags, grills, rafts, beach chairs, and groceries. I suspect these are the same adults who go to business meetings in three-story office buildings and walk a city block out of their way to find the nearest elevator, carrying only a briefcase or laptop. Many of these zealous beachgoers also bring heavy-duty shovels from home and dig five-foot-deep holes with castles, trenches, and moats that make the Biltmore House look like it was designed by an architectural dropout. I can't help but wonder if these aren't the very same people who have gardeners back home trimming their little cutesy boxwoods (they do make the best Christmas wreaths) into perfectly manicured hedges.

Avid purse carriers and excited beachgoers have something in common: We're pack rats. Since no one wants to give up pocketbooks or vacations, traveling light is not an option and bad backs are here to stay. The way I figure, only one group comes out ahead, and that's chiropractors. Oh, and the Pocketbook Manufacturers' Association. Hey, I'll bet both of these folks are probably relishing cigars and martinis at some luxury hotel bar about now, enjoying the good life while the rest of us are moaning and groaning.

Shagging After
He Left the Farm

Small steps. Hand extended, straight and steady. Upright, graceful posture and good eye contact. No, I'm not talking about teaching a baby how to walk. I'm talking about teaching your husband the shag. Or as North Carolinians call it, the bop. At least, we called it the bop back in 1964, when I learned the steps from my older sisters, Nancy and Cathy, in Jacksonville, North Carolina.

Where Russell grew up, in Pollocksville, North Carolina, population 495, those people didn't shag. Pollocksville is really small. The one and only stoplight they had was knocked down once when an eighteen-wheeler came through town. A follow-up traffic study indicated they didn't really need that traffic light after all, and it was never put back up. I hear it's still being stored in the firehouse.

Nearby Trenton—population 800, the "city" by Russell's standards as well as the county seat—was almost nothing but farm land. Future Farmers of America was the most popular club for boys at Russell's high school. Most of the girls joined Future Homemakers of America. Sports reigned supreme and was the number-one recreational activity. Russell played basketball on the local high school team. These guys would've thought learning to shag was for sissies.

I've tried to be patient and teach Russell what I could. After twenty years, he has mastered most of the important elements of the shag—all but one. It's not the small steps or the perfect posture. It's not even the rhythm, as we now have a system where I whisper, "Go up. Now go back." (Hey, y'all, forget those dance lessons; I can save you $120 if you just listen to your dance partner. That is excellent, excellent advice, if that partner is me.) This method also gives my husband full authority to say, "Ann, I can finally keep up with you."

The one smooth move that Russell can't seem to master is this: When we first get on the dance floor and hold hands, arms outstretched, he begins to grip my hand with as much force as he would if he caught a fly ball at a baseball game. Next, Russell gets to jerking his wrist up and down, up and down, and I feel like someone is wrenching my entire arm from shoulder to fingertips.

Before you know it, I'm dizzy from all that arm slinging. I plead, "Try to keep it steady," and he does. For about two minutes. Then that jerky movement takes over again and I get so confused, I forget to say, "Go up, now go back."

Without warning, he twirls me one time, I think just to have something to do—twice if he's feeling spunky. By now, I'm in mid-air and really confused. Next he steps on my toe (I've learned not to wear sandals). All the while, that arm is violently swinging up and down, making erratic half-circles.

At this point, the words to a certain song come to mind, even though the beat's too slow for shagging. It's "Rocket Man," by Elton John: *When are you going to come down? When are you going to land? I should have stayed on the farm...**

*"Rocket Man (I Think It's Going to be a Long Long Time)." Music by Elton John. Lyrics by Bernie Taupin. Honky Tonk Chateau, MCA 1611. Copyright © 1972 Dick James Music Limited.

This Chick Gets Her Kicks with Greenbax Stamps

There are two words in the English language that make me stop on a dime, eager to spend that dime and buy some groceries: Greenbax stamps. I don't know of a better bargain anywhere. I get mine at Piggly Wiggly and it's the highlight of my grocery trip.

The stamp scenario works like this: I get to the checkout and quickly unload my buggy, eager to see how much I've spent. I fumble for my keychain with the scannable thingamajigs that identify me as somebody important, and I proudly toss the cashier my PFC (Pig's Favorite Customer) card—you know the rules: no card equals no stamps—and start unloading the cart. Boxes of macaroni collide with flying frozen peas. Brillo pads and a container of vanilla ice cream tumble wildly atop the conveyor belt. Stepping back, I cast an expert eye at the heap. Concluding I am short, I toss in a few magazines. My heart starts pounding and the adrenaline starts flowing. My palms get sweaty as I nervously reach for my checkbook.

Yes, I still write checks. I know I'm in the minority. On a recent grocery stop, Katie and her cousin Maggie interrogated me for thirty minutes. Why didn't I use a debit card? Well, I'm just as sorry as I can be, but I don't know pea turkey about all that debit/credit banking nonsense, and I'm not sure I trust it. You must understand that since I've never used an ATM machine, I'll probably never use a debit card either. Sounds like an accident waiting to happen, 'cause I know I'd forget to write down how much I spent. After all, I can barely remember to put in new checks when I run out.

Back to the Gargantuan Greenbax Gala and the checkout line. As I'm standing there, I'm secretly hoping that the bill will be high. Do not tell my husband this. Sicko that I am, I know the higher the bill, the more Greenbax points I'll accumulate, and the more stuff I'll qualify for, like CD towers, silver-plated piggy banks, exercise bikes, scatter rugs, and bread machines. Maybe some of these will end up in a garage sale one day, but so what? I prefer to use the term "recycle sale," since "garage sale" has taken on a negative meaning in my house, thanks to Russell. Every time I buy anything, be it household, personal, or otherwise, he mumbles under his breath, "Probably will end up in a garage sale." Men!

The other good thing about using Greenbax stamps is that I'm carrying on a family tradition. Call me nostalgic, but I have fond memories of my mother's stamp routine in the 1960s. Sitting down to the kitchen table on a beige Naugahyde-cushioned metal chair, she would moisten the stamps using a yellow sponge. Then she'd carefully press the gummy stamps into the grids of the four-by-six-inch paper book. I can still smell the glue and picture those bulging rubber-banded books inside a cabinet over the sink, ready for redemption. Oh, and the prizes she'd redeem her stamps for: a wooden clothes hamper, bathroom scales, a steam iron. Nowadays, it's a whole new ball game. Omigosh, you can select anything from a hair-cutting kit, an eagle statue, or a mustard-seed necklace (each for five books or under), all the way to a direct-TV system (cough up 192 books) and a swivel/glider rocker (a whopping 268 books). Heck, for 866 books, you can book a flight to Hawaii and back.

In order to acquire these goodies, though, you must first earn the points. The last time I went to the Pig I didn't have my PFC card, so the manager let me use a guest card. How nice, I thought, happily writing out my one-hundred dollar check. (That's as high as I could get the total without buying two of everything.) I anxiously held out my looooong cash register tape. To my dismay, there were no additional Greenbax points added. What the heck? I nearly fell to the floor in shock. It was because (oops, naughty me) I wasn't using my permanent card. The cashier told me to bring the tape along with the card on my next visit, and she'd credit me.

Now I'm carrying around the crumpled-up receipt as if my life depended on it. I've opened my purse a dozen times since then to pay the dry-cleaner, buy postage stamps, fill my gas tank, and renew a library book, all the while guarding that precious paper. I can't wait to get back to the Pig and see my new total (it's currently eighteen books). Just think, only 848 books to go, and I'm off to Honolulu!

chapter 3

You Talk Funny, Guess You're Not Southern

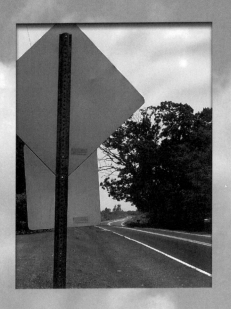

Those Taters Have Eyes and Other Sassy Southern Sayings

I was talking to someone the other day about writing a preface for this book. He agreed that I should indeed have a *farred*. "A what?" I asked. He repeated this and eventually had to just spell it. "F-o-r-e-w-o-r-d," he said. "Boy, are you Southern," I answered. I should've recognized the word because my family is as Southern as black-eyed peas and chitlins.

This next statement may not be Southern, but my mother, who, definitely *is*, loves to say, "In the first place." You know what? There never is a second place! I recently told her this, and she said, "That's why it's in the first place." Huh? Go figure.

Granny Pinky used to say, "Indeed, you are not!" This usually came after someone asked a far-out question, such as, "Granny, can I cut into that freshly baked chocolate cake you made to surprise Dad for his birthday?"

Russell has too many Southern sayings to list, but a few of my favorites are *red-ee-o* for radio, *deddy* for Daddy, and *srimp* for shrimp. Last, but not least, there's *lawn-dree* for laundry. That's how everybody talks in his hometown of Pollocksville, North Carolina.

My mother has a funny expression. When someone isn't fully dressed she says, "Liza, put your drawers on. Those sweet potatoes have eyes."

Grandma Julia had a curious word in her vocabulary: *mommuck*. As in "Don't you mommuck up that furniture!" This word is popular in North Carolina's Outer Banks. She learned it from her father, a *Hoi Toider* born and raised on Portsmouth Island.

I have a friend named Belinda whose mother has many unique sayings. I'll share two of them. She says, "I'll be to bury" if she is very upset about something. This is similar to the more common expression, "I just about died." She also says, "He is so skinny he can sit on a dime and still read 'In God We Trust.'"

Chuck Gee told me two new ones when he took my photograph the other day. He asked me if I'd ever heard of a *fartar*. I hadn't, but he gave me a hint. "Y'all come on over for a visit. We live right beside the fartar" (fire tower). Another good one was *grain sheet*. It seems Chuck was filling out papers one time and that's how the first page, a green sheet, was described to him! (He thought it was made from recycled paper—*grain?*)

The first time I ever ate at The Seafood Kitchen Restaurant in Georgetown, I called from my cell phone for directions. The woman who answered asked me where I was and politely gave me the route. The last thing she said was, "You can't miss us. We're right across the street from Dr. Tar." I am a medical transcriptionist and familiar with the local medical community, but I'd never heard of that particular doctor. Pulling up at the intersection she'd mentioned, I saw the restaurant first, and glanced across the street to see a sign that read, *Dr. Tire*.

I thought I'd heard (or said) them all, until the other night when a mosquito rode home from Myrtle Beach with us. After I'd been bitten about a dozen times (it seemed), I hollered, "I'm itching up a gum stump!" Laughing, Katie asked what in the world that meant. Then came the big shock—even Russell didn't recognize it. So, I'm doing a survey: Am I the only one in the world to use that expression? Meet me at the fartar and write your answer on the grain sheet. I'll be the one standing there waving, across from Dr. Tar.

Wild Women
Don't Get the Blues

I watched a movie at home the other night with my family, and I'll never forget one of the lines. It came from a spicy, wild-child woman who said, "Wild Women Don't Get the Blues." You know, I kind of liked that. I kind of liked that a whole lot!

My family boasts a string of wild women. I think these genes have not only been passed on through the ages, but have solidified with each generation. Take the time my sister Cathy came home from college and was struggling with a heavy, rickety Olivetti typewriter, trying to carry it up the stairs. My five-year-old daughter, Kelly, said, "Here, let me help you." She proceeded to march up that steep flight of stairs all by herself as we stood there, mouths open.

Or the summer my parents planted a garden in Bear Creek, North Carolina, where the nearest water faucet was seven-tenths of a mile away. For the first couple of weeks, before we had a good rain, my mother hauled buckets of water up the hilly dirt road each day. Her face became even redder than the humongous cherry-red tomatoes we'd grown in summers past. Each season the first crop of green tomatoes got chopped, cooked, and canned in a batch of pickled chow-chow which Mama slaved over, standing by a steaming ten-quart pot for hours at a time.

My grandparents lived out in the country, as we called it, some thirty-five miles from our "city" home in Jacksonville. (This city/country talk was comical because our hometown wasn't a city at all, compared to, say, Wilmington or Raleigh.) Grandmother Julia would stand in front of her hot stove and mix, knead, and shape two or three pans of biscuits just because we all loved them. No meal was ever served at her dining table without homemade biscuits. Her other specialties that she fixed on our Sunday visits included freshly prepared vegetables, chicken, ham, pork roast, along with a myriad of desserts. In her early years of marriage, these meals were cooked without the benefit of air conditioning. She later had a cooling unit installed.

Granny Pinky was a great cook and gardener, and she would spend hours digging in her yard, planting azaleas, crape myrtles, boxwoods, roses, and annuals and perennials. She was also an immaculate housekeeper. That kitchen floor got mopped just about every day if she had anything to do with it. She was full of energy. I never remember her watching TV without a pile of crocheting in her lap. Always doing something!

Though the above describes more strength and determination than true wildness, is there really much difference? I know in my family I was often considered the wild child, the different one, the dreamer, the strong-willed, determined, "mind-of-her-own" girl. I still am. I just finished reading Billy Baldwin's *Mrs. Whaley and Her Charleston Garden* for the umpteenth time. This fabulous book—and certainly that energetic woman—are testaments to life. I believe *Mrs. Whaley* should be required reading for high school seniors.

You see, I feel the same way as Mrs. Whaley did about life—that *it is to be lived!* She said, "A warning: Life is full of decisions and you better not waver and quaver over each one or you will stress yourself. You will die young and miss your seventies and eighties, which are two decades that can be a delight."*

Here are a few life lessons that I've learned over the years:

If it doesn't work out one way, try a different way.
If it always rains on your parade, try another parade.
Wear red! It makes people wonder about your audacity.
Give something away every day: a smile, a handshake, a prayer, an anonymous gift.
Listen to your favorite music and turn the volume up a notch higher than normal.
Be passionate!
Don't be afraid to run under the sprinkler with or without your bathing suit on.
Cut your own bangs.
Mark your calendar for the next full moon and have a "full moon party"

with yourself, the stars, a blanket, and a cappuccino.

Learn to play a musical instrument.

Start a collection (even candles from the dollar store can be classy if you think they're classy).

Let loose.

Learn to belly dance.

Read a book to a child.

Laugh at yourself and repeat an old joke to someone who's sad.

Throw a stone in a pond, or a shell into the ocean, as I often do.

Buy an ice cream cone, watch it melt, then enjoy the milkshake.

Take a nap in a hammock.

And my personal favorite: Paint your fingernails fourteen-karat gold— you're worth it.

Be wild!

And remember: "Wild Women Don't Get the Blues."

*Emily Whaley, in conversation with William Baldwin, *Mrs. Whaley and Her Charleston Garden* (Chapel Hill, NC: Algonquin Books, 1997), p. 3, 8.

Snip, Snap, or Sniff?

Sitting at a football game at Waccamaw High School the other night, proudly watching our teenagers perform in the marching band, my friends and I were discussing their family pets. Sally told me she owns a Pomeranian. "Oh," I said, "aren't they the little yippy dogs that snip?" Sally said, "Snip or snap?" At least, that's what I thought I heard her say. I asked what was the difference. Kathy, wordsmith that she is, told us, "Little dogs snip and big dogs snap." (Kathy's pet, Molly Dog, is a sweet poodle that does neither.) The real clincher came when Sally said to me, "Oh! I thought you asked if Pomeranians are the dogs that *sniff!*"

You know, some dogs are pretty darn smart. My friend Barbara has a Golden Retriever that can open doors. Her doors have fancy brass handles, and Jeffers has learned to jump up, hit the knob with his paw, and open the door. This is the really odd part: One time Barbara and her husband were outside, enjoying a beautiful day, when they realized they were locked out. After some investigating, they found out that Jeffers can now turn the deadbolt with his paw. Imagine! A dog keeping its owner from entering the house.

We tried having a dog in the Ipock household twice. The first time we bought a darling black toy poodle named Lucky. I didn't feel so lucky. She cried like a baby. In the middle of the night, I would have to walk around the house with her in my arms just to soothe her. That lasted about a month, until a friend offered to take her in. The friend's pizza delivery boy bought her for his fiancée. Then she changed homes once again. The last I heard, Lucky had flown to Ohio with a sweet tourist who had just lost an identical puppy.

A couple of years later, we tried it again. This time we decided to be a little more benevolent and drove down to the Myrtle Beach Animal Shelter. Katie picked out an energetic, fluffy blonde mix and named her Clover—as in four-leaf clover. Even with that charmed name, though, Clover wasn't so lucky either. Come to find out, she was sickly. We took her to the veterinarian, who demonstrated the best way to coax Clover into taking her pills. I tried massaging her throat, gently blowing in her face, and just plain old begging for a couple of hours, but I could see it simply was not working. I even demonstrated how to swallow, but Clover just looked at me with her head cocked. I cried, Katie cried, and for certain, Clover cried. Reluctantly, we returned her to the animal shelter with her medicine in tow, where they promised to find her another good home.

I've wondered what it is that makes some people animal lovers. That gene surely must have passed me by. I can live okay without a puppy. I prefer babies, especially my own granddaughter, Madison. In fact, raising two daughters has been the most rewarding part of my life.

I'm just glad my pet experiences with Clover and Lucky weren't a test because surely I would have failed. Snip, snap, or sniff—the whole world is not necessarily going to the dogs.

Opposites Attract...
But Don't Iron

They say, "Opposites attract." I say, "Yes, but attract what, exactly?" It's true, though, I can't argue. Russell and I are a perfect example. We couldn't be any more different. After twenty-plus years of marriage, it's for sure neither one of us is going to change. Come to think of it, that's one thing we actually do have in common.

Some of our differences are huge—for example, our temperaments. Russell is laid-back, easygoing, totally predictable, down-to-earth, and uncomplicated. I, on the other hand, am high-energy, moody, demanding, and complicated. Other differences are tolerable, and we work around them. I love to dance. He doesn't. He loves to play golf. I don't. He likes suspenseful thriller movies. I like romantic comedies. For that matter, I like romantic, candlelit, exotic dinners (especially in faraway places). Russell's response to this is usually, "I can't see what I'm eating. It's too dark in here!" In fact, that's something he and my father have in common. We once left a restaurant before even being seated because my father proclaimed he "couldn't see a thing." Another contrast: I love to garden and Russell despises even mowing the grass.

Then there is the whole entertainment scene. I enjoy visiting museums and art galleries, attending swanky fundraisers and dressy charity affairs. Russell's idea of entertainment is watching Brian Hammonds on the Golf Channel, alternately channel-surfing with ESPN, CNN, or a loud, nerve-racking TV movie.

Getting all decked out for special events is pleasurable to me. Maybe it stems back to the time when, as a teenager in the late '60s, I rode in a float for the Christmas parade in my small hometown. Dad was sponsoring the float for the Bootery Shoe Store, our family business. Mom and Dad paid for my beautiful gown, dyed-to-match *peau-de-soie* shoes, elbow-length gloves, and my hair appointment.

At that time a trip to the beauty shop meant hours of torture, including uncomfortable brush rollers, crick-in-the-neck hooded hairdryers, and a braided hairpiece woven in with my own coiffed hair, which had been teased and sprayed and teased and sprayed again. I sure felt special riding down New Bridge Street, waving to passersby and throwing candy to the little kids.

But getting back to Russell, he just plain old hates to wear a suit and tie. Now, I think I can understand and even sympathize with this. I firmly believe that twenty years of working in retail, wearing stiff, stuffy clothes, caused him to dislike getting dressed up for any occasion, special or not.

Thank God (sincerely) for Russell's new job as church administrator at First United Methodist Church in Myrtle Beach. Now he can wear those wacky Jimmy Buffet or preppy Tommy Bahama shirts, and even comfortable Savane khakis. There's just one problem though, and it didn't change with his new job. It's one of the rare things we have in common: He hates to iron and so do I.

Two Heads (But Not Two Names) Are Better than One

What is it with Southern country-folk giving babies two names (normal) but calling them by both of them (not normal)? Whenever we'd go visit Russell's mother in rural North Carolina, she'd give us the town news, condensed into a two-hour version: "Did I tell you that Sudie Mae's back went out and she had to travel clear to Kinston to see that new bone doctor? How about Edward Earl closing down his store? Oh, Betty Jo said to tell you she's been busy planning your high school reunion."

In my case, I'm glad no one ever called me Margaret Ann, my given name—except for Clyde Hurst in high school, and he finally shortened it to Maggie, just to tease me. That's okay. I got even by calling him Farnell, his middle name.

Names have always fascinated me. As a writer, I keep a file on them. When I worked for a finance company years ago, I discovered two of our customers had noble-sounding names. One was named Lawyer and the other, Governor. These names are really listed on their birth certificates, they tell me.

Anyway, I know Katie is glad she was born a girl. If she had been a boy, Russell was determined to name him William Robert. That in itself wasn't too bad, but I threw a fit when he said, "We'll call him Billy Bob for short." As Granny Pinky would've said, "Indeed you are not!"

Nicknames can be just as bad as double names. I once knew a woman named Tiny who weighed close to 300 pounds. I also knew a man named Stick who weighed about 120 pounds, and was quite tall. I have a friend whose best friend is married to a man named Fatty. And we've all heard the classic Southern debutante names, such as Muffy, Buffy, Biffy, Sissy, and Cammie. For me, these names conjure up a vision of Scarlett O'Hara at Tara Hall.

I realize we can't choose our last names. If you're burdened with one like Hock (a family that lives near me) you're just stuck—but, please, parents, don't pick an absurd first name like Holly. That child will be teased by mocking classmates. After all, look at poor Rose-anne Rosanna Danna (who I'm sure was picked on with that name). There's one thing Rosanne and I have in common—our grand-mothers used to have a lot of sayings. Granny Pinky used to say, "You can call me anything you want. Just don't call me late for din-ner." Come to think of it, it's time for dinner, so I better stop writing. Everybody is getting hungry, and I think I'll go bake up some Julia Margaret biscuits, named for my other grandmother. She is also the mother of Emmie Lou and Betty Rae.

You Wouldn't Understand, It's a Shopping Thing

It happened again. Only, this time I was the one who got lost in a shopping center. I'm beginning to see a pattern here, involving mega-stores and/or malls that have multiple doors.

A while back I wrote a column about losing my sister Cathy in Lowe's. Why did this happen, you ask? Lowe's had multiple doors, which I traversed in and out of many times that day, looking for my sister. Finally, I had her paged. I'll bet most of the bystanders expected Cathy to be a mere child, perhaps my daughter. Rarely does a woman lose her grown sister inside a store.

The second occasion on which I lost kinfolk not only included my sister Cathy, but also my sister Nancy and my mom at Kohl's Department Store in Raleigh. While we all stood there, paying for our merchandise, I noticed Cathy was holding some darling creme-colored sandals. Funny thing was, I had spent about fifteen minutes looking for shoes earlier, and found nothing. But, oh, these sandals were perfect! The right color, the right style, and the right price—and I wanted some.

I told the three of them I'd go look for a pair for me, but that I'd be right back. I wasn't away five minutes (no luck on footwear) and when I came back, you guessed it. They were gone. All three of them —vanished—just like that. "Well, I never! They sure are impatient," I huffed under my breath.

Now, keep in mind, the store was crowded with anxious bargain hunters pushing buggies in every direction. You could barely see the tile floor below your feet. Every register was being utilized, and there were long lines at each checkout counter.

I found a semi-quiet corner out of the way of the confusion and decided to call Nancy on her cell phone. My plan was to ask her to have Cathy find those sandals in my size. The only problem was, I couldn't remember Nancy's cell phone number. I called Russell, who was at Nancy's house with her husband, Keith, and asked for the number. Well, as luck would have it, someone at the house had her on the line. I relayed the message to give to her, but she'd hung up before they could tell her. Now that I had her cell number, I dialed it, but the phone wouldn't ring.

It was a beautiful, clear day and quite hot. I went outside and patiently stood, confident that one of them was looking out for me, as they (I presumed) sat in Nancy's Toyota, waiting. No one came. I heard a car honk, but couldn't tell where it came from. Then a Toyota backed out of a space and headed toward me, but it wasn't hers. I was beginning to feel a little foolish.

Finally I couldn't stand it anymore. I called Nancy's cell phone again, and this time she answered. I said heatedly, "Could I please have a ride home?" She replied, "Where are you?" Then I really got miffed. I figured she'd driven on home because she couldn't find me. "I'm standing here at Kohl's waiting for you. Y'all left me!"

Now Nancy was puzzled. "Where at Kohl's?" she asked. "On the sidewalk, what's the difference? Where are *you*?" I said in my most sisterly-sarcastic voice. "Right behind you," she answered. I turned around and we both laughed. We were about forty feet apart, each standing at a set of double doors.

We got in the car and all four of us started talking at once, trying to figure out exactly where we'd gone wrong. It turns out that as I was making my purchase, Cathy realized she still had a dress on (the store's, that is). The tags were even hanging out, but no one else noticed. She had experienced what I call, "Shop til you drop, and you'll end up in a trance" syndrome. Surely you women out there have gone through this: You've shopped so long that you've forgotten about dinner, your husband or significant other, the store rules, your name, and whether or not you even own a car. When Cathy went to change back into her own outfit, her clothes had vanished. She eventually discovered that someone had removed them, folded them, and placed them by the dressing room door, on the floor.

In the meantime, Nancy and Mom were waiting for her at the register where they had already paid and where Cathy would eventually make her purchase.

Now I saw how we'd lost each other: While I was standing at the north exit paying, they were standing at the south exit paying. To make matters worse, while Nancy and Mom were waiting for Cathy to change her clothes, I'd walked outside.

Now I think I understand why Russell left the retail business. All those crazy women getting lost, merchandise almost getting removed from the store while personal clothes stayed behind, and last but not least, sibling rivalry. It's a shopping thing!

The Girls' Trip Away
(You Go, Girl!)

I highly recommend that all you women out there go on an annual
girls' trip. I think that's where the term, "You go, girl!" originated.
I just got back from one, and I'm here to tell you, it was a riot. It
doesn't matter if you're reading *Redbook*, playing Taboo, or reminisc-
ing about those good old high school days (*"You never told me you
kissed Ronald Mundy!"*), you've left your worries at home, and you're
spending quality time with friends.

For more than ten years, six of my old friends, my sister Nancy,
and I have had an annual get-together. Our last trip included makeovers, redecorating (on paper) our friend's condo, and discovering a
new game, Bop-It. We've battled heat waves, Christmas shopping
stampedes, gold-necklaced flirty men in tight shirts, confusing one-
way streets, nausea from overeating chocolate and Chili Con Queso,
and other annoyances. We're not the Ya-Yas, but we do call ourselves
the Royal Highnesses. (Madelene declared herself the Mad Queen
and named me the Ant Queen—a variation of our first names.)

We usually go somewhere interesting: Myrtle Beach (where I
play tour guide), Wrightsville Beach, Raleigh, or Topsail Island. Our
last trip (at Judy's "camp") was in the middle of nowhere; I don't even
think the town had a name! It was beautiful: serene, quaint, and at
the top of a hill with a small body of water below.

Thankfully, none of our outings has been as bizarre as the "Trip
of '99." Only three of us could make the journey. We rented a condo in North Myrtle Beach. The weekend went from bad to worse.
The first night Madelene fussed at me for bringing thirteen pairs
of shoes (for a three-day trip), and I fussed at her for carrying an
industrial-sized suitcase on wheels.

We went out to dinner. When we got back, we realized we had
forgotten to leave on the porch light. Worse than that, the screen
door was wide open. All three of us were sure we had shut it before

we left. Madelene asked, "You think someone is in there?" I peeked through the glass panel beside the door and saw an unfamiliar black boot lying on the floor. Shaking all over, I said, "D-d-d-did anyone bring boots on this trip?" They yelled in unison, "No!"

We crept inside, and Madelene picked up a candlestick. "What are you doing?" Pam inquired. (She's the level-headed one.) "If anyone is in here, I'm going to let them have it." Madelene shook the candlestick at us, and the candle fell to the floor. "Rats," she said, realizing the fake brass candlestick only weighed about one ounce.

Pam ran toward the mystery boot. When she got close enough to have a good look, she sighed with relief. "This is not a boot, y'all." It turned out to be a leather shoe with a sock lying beside of it at a ninety-degree angle.

Still, we were nervous. Everyone was afraid to sleep alone, so Pam, Madelene, and I ended up in one double bed, for protection. We were packed in there like sardines, and I didn't dare roll over or move all night. After staring at the ceiling for eight hours, I had neck cricks and back spasms. To add insult to injury, Madelene woke up at 5:30 a.m. (early bird that she is) smiling and singing, "Okay girls, nothing got us. Let's get up and get going!" I was ready to fling her inside her humongous suitcase (there was room for her) and zip it up. Luckily, Pam the Peacemaker refereed the fight, and as they say, "All's well that ends well."

That day we shopped until our feet ached, read novels until our eyes crossed, and stuffed ourselves with all-you-can-eat crab legs and dessert until we wobbled away, a few pounds heavier. Coming back exhausted, we forgot about the previous night's scare. We said good-night and went into our individual bedrooms. (I think Madelene kept her light on.) Then we all collapsed into our respective roomy beds, feeling secure, ready to ponder next year's girls' trip away.

You Made Your Bed, Now Lie (Not Nap) in It

Raise your hand if you've bought or shopped for a new bed lately. Gosh, I've never had so many choices in my life: inner coil, twelve-gauge steel, tighter weave in the middle, pipe-like reinforcements on the sides, a sewn-in feather topper, silky shiny material, extra firm or soft, king, queen, or twin, etc. (Besides, what's with the king, queen, or twin? Why isn't it king, queen and prince/princess?) The more questions I asked, the more confused I got.

When we first drove into the parking lot, I told Russell, "Don't even look at the beds in the window at the front of the store. That selection features the highest-priced ones. The store owners might think they are fooling us, but they're not."

We walked in and a friendly gentleman came up and asked us if he could help. Since Russell likes for me to do the talking, I did. I explained that we wanted a basic mattress, fairly firm, queen-size, and in a moderate price range. He took us to the back of the store, saying he had exactly what we wanted. After we tried out three beds, he said, "Of course, if it was me, I'd go for something more like these." He showed us six beds in ten minutes, and before we knew it we found ourselves at the front of the store, standing next to the row of expensive beds.

Russell must have misunderstood the man who waited on us. Although the salesman did say to test all the beds we liked, he didn't mean for us to TAKE A NAP, which is exactly what Russell tried to do. One difference between men and women: A woman lies down on a new mattress in a store and immediately says, "Nope, too soft," then goes on to the next option. A man tosses and turns, lies on his back, rolls onto his side, bends his knees into a fetal position, and just gets comfortable in general. About the fifth bed along, I peeked back at Russell and found him snoring in the first bed we'd tested! A lot of help he was.

I had nearly settled on my selection when darned if that salesman didn't start talking about futons and electric beds. After that, he mentioned iron headboards and middle-support frames. At this point, I began to fade. Even though I could see a man's face, watch his body motioning, and hear muffled noises, I was weary from his descriptions and explanations. All I wanted was to buy a mattress. Period. My mind wandered, and then I could only visualize myself going straight home and straight to bed (my old one) from sheer exhaustion.

Eventually, we narrowed it down to front-row beds. I told the clerk I wanted the Empress. (Isn't that a Carnival Cruise Line ship?) Sounded good to me. The bed was comfortable and fairly priced. I especially liked the swirly gold-and-ivory printed fabric. Plus, this "upper-end" row had matching tapestry-pillow shams, which I loved. I thought, *Aha! This will be my bargaining chip.* I told him we'd made our selection and would he throw in the pillows for good measure? Not hardly, he told me; they weren't for sale.

Thirty minutes after arriving, we walked out of the store with a front-row bed. Russell was happy (he got in his thirty-minute nap). I got the middle support legs, but no pillows. Oh, well, they say you can't have everything, and I guess it's true.

My Dad's Gone Psychi

My father is psychic. There, I said it. Now I feel better. I admit this sounds strange, but really it's not. In fact, Dad is using his newfound talent in positive ways and I, for one, am benefiting. In a matter of one month, Dad made two predictions that came true: Where I'd find my lost diamond ring, and where I would meet a new friend, many miles from home.

As I was getting ready for bed one night, I realized my favorite piece of jewelry was missing. After I'd finished my computer work, I went to pick up my two rings off the desk, like I do every night. (I take them off when I type because they're uncomfortable.) Only one was there—the gold cigar band. The diamond dinner ring was gone. Both gifts were given to me by Russell in honor of our wedding anniversaries.

To complicate matters, Russell had vacuumed the house earlier that evening. As I began to search, I could imagine the ring inside a thick wad of dust, lint, string, fibers—along with whatever else the vacuum cleaner had sucked up. I told this to Russell. He assured me that wasn't possible because he would have heard the metal rattling around inside the machine. This is the same man that says "huh?" fifty times a night during dinner conversation.

I decided to begin an all-out exploration. First I moved everything off the desk, including my LaserJet printer. Next I searched behind the desk and under my chair. As a last resort, I felt around the bookshelf, rearranging books, baskets, knickknacks, candles, and picture frames. Nada. I got down on my hands and knees and felt every square inch of Berber carpet. I began sweating. How could a ring just disappear?

Feeling defeated, I went to bed with plans to re-search the whole house early the next morning. I barely slept, and as soon as daylight began filling the bedroom, I jumped up. After one last inspection of every room in the house, I decided to check the vacuum cleaner.

The vacuum doesn't have a bag, but rather a filter, so I could see the trash through the clear window. Our new Eureka Whirlwind Big Cup Bagless Cyclonic (who names these things anyway?) was indeed ringless. Not giving up, I shook the vacuum cleaner vigorously, then attempted to take it apart. Because I couldn't locate even one screw, I scrapped that idea. Finally, I plugged it in, turned it upside down, and nearly lost my hand when I accidentally touched the beater bar.

Later that day, Dad called me from his home in North Carolina. He could tell when I answered that something was wrong, and he asked me about it.

"Oh, Dad, I'm just sick! I've lost my diamond ring."

"You'll find it," he said. "It's probably in some paper or inside a book."

Do what? I asked Dad to repeat himself. It didn't even sound like his voice. As we continued talking, I made my way down the hall toward the living room. Sure enough, I spotted the shiny band inside a book, protruding only a quarter-inch or so. At that moment everything seemed surreal, like I was in a slow-motion movie. As I stepped forward and opened the book, my hands were shaking. The ring fell out. Dad was still on the phone and I yelled, "You're not going to believe this…"

Dad's second psychic experience occurred when Russell and I went on a cruise to the Caribbean. We were boarding the ship and I called my parents from my cell phone. Dad proclaimed immediately, "I'll bet you'll meet a neighbor from Pawleys Island on your trip." I told him I didn't think so because when I had spoken with Delena, my travel planner at *Southern Living* Travel Services, she told me we were the only ones on her list from Pawleys.

The first night at sea we sat among four-hundred-plus guests in the dining room. We were assigned tablemates who said they were from Kentucky, and we told them where we were from. All of a sudden, this cheerful, animated lady popped her head out from behind a partition at her booth and said to me, "You're from Pawleys Island? Well, so am I! I'm Alice Harrelson."

Come to find out, Alice's daughter, Mandie, is from Florence, South Carolina. Mandie had made travel arrangements for herself, her mother, and her daughter, Allison. That's why my planner had no record of a guest from our town. I thought back to my dad's prediction, and felt a slight chill.

I can't help but wonder what are the odds of meeting my neighbor among 2000 passengers on the Carnival Pride cruise ship. The fact that this was the first night of our vacation, and she sat right beside us, is even stranger. As it turns out, she lives about four miles from my house, and we've kept in touch since coming home.

I'm not sure when or how Dad acquired his psychic powers, but I'm glad he did. Since he's helped me find an old ring and discover a new friend, I'm feeling pretty lucky. I can't wait to hear his next prediction—I think I'll give him a call right now.

Does the Song Say, "I'm No Fool" (And How Would I Know)?

Insomnia is my middle name and I've always had some form of it, ever since I can remember. When I was a little girl, maybe four or five, doctors didn't prescribe sleeping medication to children.

I'm sure I was a real pain because I didn't nod off easily at bedtime. I'd ask for water, complain about hearing a noise, or just plead to be allowed to get up and play.

My mother likes to tell the story of the time I sleepwalked. It was an isolated incident, as far as I know. My parents were having a couple of tables of bridge that night, and I walked into the living room and just stopped, facing the wall. I didn't say a word. I would imagine that was pretty strange for the guests (and my parents). Mama gently walked me back to my room and tucked me into bed.

Another time when I was about three years old, I managed to get out of bed, open the back door, go outside, and start playing on the swing set. Mama said she heard me calling her name, waking her from a sound sleep. She ran into my bedroom, but I was not in my bed. Finally she realized the back door was open. She ran outside in the pitch black and brought me back inside.

As an adult I am only plagued with insomnia (no more sleepwalking or playing outdoors at midnight). Thank goodness there's help in the form of exercise, biofeedback, and when all else fails, modern medicine.

Since my doctor has been treating me with a very mild sleeping medication, I've gotten more rest, more sound sleep, and more REM than I ever remember. My daughter Katie says I get a little weird right before I doze off each night. She'll come into my bedroom as I'm drifting. The next day, she'll tell me all the wacky things I've said.

One night when she turned off my light, I turned to her and

sweetly said, "You're a beauty queen." Once I described in vivid detail a "red-and-black-and-black" kitchen I'd like to own, complete with gold-legged barstools. I went on to say that there would be tassels on the menus and tassels on the chairs. Now excuse me, but I can't remember the time I've ever displayed menus at my own kitchen table or employed a wait staff (which I've also described in detail to Katie).

The other night Geneva, Katie's friend, came over to cut my daughter's hair. Geneva is so talented I like to tell her she could be an actress (she played Shelby in "Steel Magnolias" alongside my Truvy). She's also wonderful with makeovers; from time to time, reinventing a friend's style with a new hairdo, makeup, or wardrobe.

Anyway, this particular night Katie and Geneva waited until I was almost asleep, and then they tried to pry information from me. I don't know if I believe them, but they say at one point I made up lyrics to a country song! Guess what? They didn't write them down.

Just think, I could be in Nashville this time next week pitching a hit to Garth Brooks. I wonder if it went something like this:

I'm a fool to wait until I sleep
to sing a song that I can't keep.
I'm a fool to let them say
I wrote a song they just won't play.
I'm a fool to even believe
I can wear my feelings on my (pajama) sleeve.

Well, *excuse me*, but I have to go to bed now to think up something I won't remember tomorrow...

No, Virginia, There Is No Oat Cheese

When we moved to the Lowcountry thirteen years ago, my primary goal was to visit every restaurant within a fifty-mile radius. As the area has grown (and so have I from that good cooking) I've realized I may never accomplish my goal. But I do keep trying. And because we eat out often, I've witnessed a few mishaps.

For instance, one night Russell and I were dining at a restaurant in Myrtle Beach. The place was new, so we were being tolerant of the slow service. We had an appetizer, drank our tea, and munched on the bread. Lots of locals were there, and we got up to speak to a couple of friends at one point. Finally, the waitress came over and asked if there was anything else we needed. "How about our meal?" Russell asked. She laughed. "Yeah, right. Seriously, do you need anything else?" Her face turned from white to red (even her ears turned red) after we explained that we had not been given our meal. She stuffed the bill into her pocket and ran back to the kitchen.

I believe that restaurant miscommunications occur more frequently than most people realize. Many years ago, my sister Nancy and I were at a diner in my parents' hometown. The waitress took our order and then asked Nancy, "Would you like Super Juice?" Nancy stammered, "I don't know." She looked at me and I repeated the words, "Soup or juice?" Nancy blinked several times. The woman shifted her weight, put her hand on her hip, and slowly asked again through clenched teeth, "Soup—or—juice?"

Along those same lines, when Katie was three years old, a waiter asked if she'd like soup or salad, and she said, "Okay." The waiter asked which one, and Katie said, "Super." At a Japanese restaurant where they cook tableside, the chef asked Russell, Kelly, and me how we'd like our steak cooked. "Medium," we each responded. When it came to be Katie's (then four years old) turn, she exclaimed, "Large!"

Recently, I heard about some other restaurant-hoppers who'd

had an interesting experience. Apparently there was a couple who had been to many different dining establishments during their one-week vacation in Myrtle Beach. They decided to attend service at a local church before heading back home later that day. When the usher approached, asking where they would prefer to sit, they said without thinking, "Non-smoking, please."

Things can get mixed up, all right. When Kelly came home one night, she brought me a to-go box from a popular Italian restaurant. "It's shrimp alfredo and it'd be good for your lunch tomorrow," she said. The next day I picked up the container to heat it. To my dismay, a pork chop lay inside. This was not Kelly's meal. It was some stranger's half-eaten food, complete with teethmarks on half a roll. Gross! Whoever ate my lunch that day, I hope you enjoyed it.

This last tale is about my dear cousin Claye Frank and his wife, Virginia. Virginia is originally from Virginia, where they pronounce the word *out* as *oat*. While living in North Carolina, they once ate at a restaurant where Virginia ordered a "hamburger without cheese." With her Southern Virginian drawl, it sounded like, "I'd like a hamburger with oat cheese." After some time, the waiter came out and said he'd never heard of oat cheese, the cook had never heard of it, and the owner had never heard of it. "What is oat cheese?" he asked.

Exasperated, Virginia looked around the restaurant. Just then a customer in the next booth began rearranging his burger platter. He lifted the bun, exposing a thick slab of golden, melted cheese. Then he poured ketchup atop his steaming cheeseburger. Virginia could make her point. She pointed to the gentleman's meal. "That," she proudly exclaimed to the waiter, "is exactly what I don't want." "No ketchup it is," the waiter said, and walked away.

Virginia and Claye recently retired to Tennessee. She now orders her meal as follows: "I'd like a hamburger, hold the cheese, please."

Real Southern Ladies
Don't Use Toothpicks

I was having lunch with a friend the other day when the subject of nails came up. No, not the kind of nails you hammer in the wall. I'm talking about fingernails. This friend said she had to get going because she was having her nails done. I looked down at her hands and said, "Ooooh, let me see." However, she wouldn't show me. She actually balled up her fists and hid them behind her back, saying, "Don't look. I bite them down to the quick once a year whenever I have a harrowing experience, and then have to get them redone." Doesn't that beat all? I thought, *If she only has one harrowing experience a year, she's darned lucky*. I have about three a week. But about nails…

Been there, done that. I tried fake nails—for a solid year—and I couldn't stand it. They drove me crazy. You notice I said fake nails, because let's be honest, that's what they are. Fake. I realize lots of prissy women say acrylic nails, fiberglass nails, gel nails. Whatever. Give me a break, they're still fake.

True, I did feel oh-so feminine and ultra-chic during my fake-nail reign. When I walked into Time Warner to pay my bill only seconds after my initial application (that's nail talk for when I first had 'em done), the lady at the counter exclaimed, "Oh, your nails are beautiful!" In fact, I heard that a lot. It's the one thing that kept me coming back for fill-ins (more nail talk) every two weeks. Positive reinforcement does it every time. Oh, and I loved picking out new colors at the end of the appointment: Corvette Red, 24K Gold. Such names kind of made me want to try them all.

However, my newfound beauty was not without its problems. The first time I had the fake nails applied, I came home and found out I couldn't do a thing. Couldn't dig in the dirt and plant my new annuals. Couldn't reach into my wallet and get change to buy extra copies of the *Georgetown Times* (for family out of state who read my column). But the worst and most humiliating part was getting food stuck in my teeth and not being able to remove it with my pinky nail. For instance, soon after acquiring the new nails, I ate a slice of delicious lemon pound cake made with tiny black poppyseeds. One of the seeds got stuck between my two front teeth, and I tried to extract it with my pinky nail as usual—but this proved impossible. Hard as I tried, my thick new nail could no longer squeeze into the tight space between my teeth.

Russell and I were dining with my parents the night *it* happened. I stooped to an all-time low, hitting rock bottom as a Southern Lady, when we were leaving the restaurant. I picked up a toothpick from the silver roll-out dispenser. That's right, right there at the Mai Tai cash register, in front of the throng of waiting diners. Dad stared at me in horror. "You're not really going to?" I smiled, tight-lipped. He shook his head and pleaded, "Not in public!" I thought he was going to cry.

Now, please understand, I'm not making fun of the nail industry. Heck, my father owns a strip mall in eastern North Carolina, and one of his tenants is Tweed Nails. The whole staff there is just fabulous. Tweed herself has done my nails (my real nails, a manicure) and I loved the whole experience. It's a good place to catch up on the latest news, learn about the hippest fashion trends, as well as people-watch. Just once, though, I'd like to be a fly on the wall and see how in the world determined nail-enthusiasts remove menacing food particles from their mouths.

Honey, I don't care how gorgeous your clothes look, how fabulous your shoes are, how impressive your jewelry is, or how precious your hairstyle seems. If you're standing there smiling, with spinach wedged between your two front teeth, trust me, that's all anyone will notice!

Forty-Something,
Foolish, and Free

A few years back my husband and I decided it was time to trade in our old blue Chevrolet Cavalier. It had been a pretty good car, but was becoming more and more expensive to keep up. During the Thanksgiving holidays, my two daughters and I decided to check out a few car lots.

Kelly volunteered to drive her new Honda, thinking the salespeople wouldn't be so aggressive, and we wouldn't look like pushovers. We tried to sneak up and park at the side of the showroom. Big mistake. Kelly has a heavy foot, and she drove right up to the building—right up, as in touching it. As her car's bumper bounced off the concrete, not one but all of the salesmen ran out. "Can we help you?" they asked, really meaning it. We smiled as Kelly put the car in reverse and backed up a couple of feet into the designated parking space.

I get nervous when we buy cars, and since we already had everyone's attention and we looked a little clueless, I was not in a good mood. I think the car salesman knew that my mental status was altered, what with the near-crash and all. He proceeded to talk me into test-driving a sleek, candy-apple red Mitsubishi Eclipse. We three girls rode around the parking lot a while. Then, at my request, the salesman made a call to the owner of the dealership (who was our friend), and he offered us the car for the weekend.

I drove off that lot feeling euphoric. I was dangerous. I never knew how much fun you could have with a little red sports car—taking those sharp curves on two wheels, goosing it (a term from my high-school days) from speeds of zero to sixty in ten seconds flat, zipping in and out of traffic. I sat low but I felt high. Wow! This baby had power, charm, and good looks. Plus, the price was right.

I drove straight to my husband's office, calling him first to say, "Meet me out front. I've got a surprise." He just stood there shaking his head. I expected him to tell me to drive right back over there and turn it in. Had I lost my mind? Was I going through a mid-life crisis? Did I know what I was doing? Instead he said, "Move over."

"What?" I asked him.

"Move over. I want to drive."

Russell did all the things I'd done and more. He rolled down the window and hung his arm out. He opened the sunroof and let his salt-and-pepper hair fly in the wind. He turned up the Beach Boys so the music blasted out of the quadraphonic stereo speaker. Then he did something really neat. He put on his sunglasses and cruised down Ocean Boulevard. He was hooked, too.

When I told Russell we had the car for a three-day weekend, I thought he would never give me back the keys. That whole weekend we took turns driving. I even let Kelly get behind the wheel, but only on the back streets, and only with me in the passenger's seat.

There was one dilemma though. When our lanky eleven-year-old, Katie, climbed in the backseat, her knees touched her chin. She never complained and it seemed manageable at the time, so we kept "test-driving" the car. We rode all around showing it to our friends and getting their approval. "Wow! I think you should get it," most everyone said. "We are," Russell assured them.

But in the end, I chickened out. We talked it over and agreed. There was no leg room. When six-foot-two Russell got behind the wheel, the backseat got even smaller. It didn't help matters that he had to lie down before he got in the car and then roll to the ground to get out.

Space was cramped. Even when she sat behind my seat, Katie's legs crumpled up like an accordion. The trunk wouldn't hold a suitcase and golf clubs at the same time, and Russell never goes out of town without his golf clubs. Then there was the cost of insurance. Lastly, an emergency room doctor-friend reminded me that more people have accidents driving red sports cars than any other type of vehicle. Like I said, I got chicken and Russell got practical.

The day we returned the car, the salesman tried every trick he knew to sell us the Eclipse. It was no use. He showed us car after car. Bleary-eyed, exhausted and numb, we ended up with a Mitsubishi all right, but a Mitsubishi black truck. It was everything the Eclipse was not. It had no power steering, no power windows, five speeds that stuck, a hard, crusty seat, and a radio that didn't work. On the positive side, there was lots of leg room, it was a safer choice, and it was cheaper to insure—plus cheaper to buy. Also, it had a bed to haul around pine straw, mismatched furniture, and other assorted novelties.

The weekend I was forty-something, foolish, and free made me realize we have choices. Sometimes practicality wins out and it did this time. But just think: In another five years Katie will be driving her own car (maybe my Cavalier) and I'll buy my dream car. The biggest difference between then and now is I'll be forty-something, sensible, and free.

chapter 4

General Observations from the Nut House

Hold Your Tongue and Forget the Gum

I've decided this world is full of two kinds of people: gum lovers and non-gum lovers. I am a non-gum lover and there's a reason for that. In fact, I forbid (Queen's command) gum in my home.

Russell rarely chews gum. When he does, he chomps with his mouth open and then assumes a fixed stare, unaware of anyone or anything around him. He makes horrible sounds like *schmmmmm, clmmmmmppp, brmmmmgg*. It drives me crazy!

Used to be we'd go on a car trip to North Carolina, and I'd get together a goody bag full of candy, mints, and gum. Then I discovered that annoying habit of his. Now not only do I not buy gum, I hide it if I find any.

One time Russell was going to town (so to speak) on that gum. I mean, really giving it everything he had, when he suddenly said, "Oh no!" Two hours later in the Emergency Room, they told us they cannot stitch up a tongue. Keep that in mind if you have the same tendency toward violent chewing. His split tongue finally quit bleeding, but he couldn't talk right for a week. When he asked me if I had any aspirin or an ice pack, it came out so garbled that, bless his heart, I just couldn't help him at all. (Have you ever seen anyone put an ice pack on their tongue?)

Gum isn't the only dangerous treat. Both of my daughters, Kelly and Katie, crave sweets. When Katie and I headed out with our friends Suzanne and Stefani for the long drive to All-State band competition last year, each mother-daughter team had its own bags of candy. I passed out Tic Tacs (the orange ones are my favorite). I love to ask, "What's your favorite color of Tic Tac? And what's your Tic Tac quota?" Everyone has an opinion! My answers are orange and two. Anyway, I choked on my Tic Tac and coughed and sputtered for a few seconds while everyone prepared to do the Heimlich "remover," as Katie called it at age four.

I groaned, "Oooooh," as the tears streamed down my cheeks, "it burns going down!" Ten minutes later when we stopped to get gas, I looked down, and there was that menacing Tic Tac stuck to my collar. I felt like a fool. Heck, I was one!

I guess the moral of this story is that you cannot choke on a Tic Tac you didn't swallow, and there's an art to chewing gum—elegantly, silently, and courteously. It's just that no one has ever learned how to chew it that way, and I'm sure it's not nearly as much fun.

Bathroom Break: It's No Longer Just a Woman Thing

Never again will I let a man say to me, "It's a woman thing," when I go to the restroom to powder my nose. As of October 30, 1999, it's a *man* thing. At the risk of embarrassing four cool-dude macho men—otherwise known as the Prop Pops: Joe, Jay, Dru, and Russell—here's the story: The Prop Pops are several fathers of band students from Waccamaw High School Marching Band who design, build, and set up the props for band competition. On this infamous day, we rode in a caravan of three vehicles going to Newberry, South Carolina, to see the state championship.

We were cruising along comfortably at about seventy-five miles per hour when the leader of the pack (Joe was driving the school's brand new trailer) pulled off into a truck stop. "Why are we stopping?" I asked Russell. "Probably Dru has to go the bathroom." "Do what?" I said. Russell explained that he'd ridden with Dru to another competition, and Dru had stopped often for bathroom breaks.

When we travel in the Ipock car, we never stop for anything. The entire family gets quizzed about eighty-four times, just before we walk out the door, as we settle into the car, and finally at the end of the driveway: "Did everyone go to the bathroom?" If the answer's no, we swing right back into the garage and wait until everyone goes.

Dru must not follow the same pre-travel drill, since he had to go. That's the only reason Joe would have pulled over (he's even more antsy on road trips than we are). Of course, Jay followed suit in his truck—and then us in our Buick. Before I could say lickety-split, four men had disappeared. Okay, I thought, guess I'll take advantage of this situation, too, and off I went to the women's room. While I was in there, I spotted a machine with a sign that read, "Get your weight and your lucky number." So I did. My numbers were 127 and 485, and I'm not saying which was which.

When a lady came out of a stall behind me I asked her to weigh herself, just to see if the scale was accurate. I even provided the quarter for her to use. She stepped on the scale and beamed, saying, "It's exactly right. It says 217 and that's what I weigh." I asked her what her lucky number was, and she looked at me like I was crazy.

When I came outside, the guys were standing around, looking sheepish, buying snacks to cover up the real reason we'd stopped. I teased them, saying, "You guys had to go to the bathroom! Wow! You're worse than kids." Jay waved a pack of Oreos at me. Dru stirred his gallon-size mega-cup coffee deal. (Honestly, didn't the man realize that's why we'd had to stop barely an hour-and-a-half into the trip?) Russell stood there with a pack of peanuts, and Joe left without a word. Someone said he'd stopped to get ice. Yeah, right.

So then we walked out to the parking lot, and guess what! There was a twenty-two-foot horse trailer, and coming from it was the sound of barking. Honest. Jay and I figured at that point we were in the Twilight Zone, and we both asked the logical question: "If they can teach horses to bark, can they teach dogs to gallop?" I don't know about that, but I wish someone would teach men how to potty before they leave home.

Long Live the Romay!

Last Saturday was a sad day in the Ipock household. Thank heavens this was not due to the loss of a friend or family member, certainly not the loss of a pet (we are pet-less) and not poor health or finances. No, I am talking about the dearly departed Romay hair-brush that Russell said goodbye to without so much as a "You did a good job, and I'm going to miss you." I was getting ready for play practice of *Other People's Money* when Russell entered our bedroom and announced, "Well, I'm getting rid of my hairbrush." I had to sit down. I thought I'd heard him wrong. I never thought I'd see the day.

You have to understand, Russell has had the same seafoam-green plastic-handled Romay hairbrush since I met him twenty-plus years ago. The one with the black boar's bristles and the accumulation of salt-and-pepper gray hairs. To me the brush was an interesting antique, the symbol of an era; to him, a used-up accessory that had stood the test of time.

I tried to appeal to his sense of decency. "You'll never find another one like it." His rebuttal was, "Sure I will. I'll go look tomorrow." Then I tried to make him feel guilty. "Honey, now just think about it. This brush has been there for you, through good times and bad. Through Little League baseball games, junior high dances, our own wedding, and all the years in between." It was no use. He had Kelly Tilghman clicked on the TV Golf Channel before I'd even finished my little spiel.

A couple of days later, I had to run out to Sally's Beauty Supply for hair spray and shampoo. I thought it was a bit odd that he insisted on riding with me. This man hates to shop. He would rather roll around naked in a briar patch than step one foot in a store. The exception to the rule is Piggly Wiggly, for some odd reason. Must be those delicious cappuccinos we get from the deli. Anyway, I was getting ready to write a check at Sally's, but Russell was nowhere to be found. Come to find out he was slinking around the hairbrush bin, picking up brushes of various sizes, colors, and materials. He didn't say a word. He didn't have to. Neither did I. He just smiled at me, proceeded to the counter, and shucked out $2.95 for a black-handled, impersonal, molded plastic hairbrush with those itty bitty barbell-looking things at the end of the bristles.

Oh sure, this brush had a few fancy gimmicks, such as a little hole in the end to hang it up and a rubber handle with molded finger grooves. Some might even call that thing cool, but it certainly didn't have the class or character of the Romay.

Know what? Just now I ran down the hall to his bathroom to find the new hairbrush so I could describe it. I opened the drawer, and there it was, right beside the Romay! I guess Russell couldn't bring himself to throw away the old standby.

It might be a good idea for me to dash off a letter to Paul Rice, who writes that antique appraisal Q&A newspaper column. Who knows? He might tell me the Romay is worth five thousand dollars. Oops, maybe I'm brushing my hair a little too hard myself. Do you think my brain is softening up?

Regardless, long live the Romay!

Ode to Snoring and Puffing

I have one of the nicest husbands in the world. He is a kind, generous, big-hearted, slow-moving, easygoing Southerner who won my heart because of these very qualities. But when I married him, he failed to mention one trait to me. He snores. Actually, he doesn't merely snore. He parts curtains. He wakes up the sleeping birds outside our window. He makes odd and frightening noises.

To complicate matters, Russell falls asleep in about three seconds once his head hits the pillow—and sometimes before it hits the pillow. I, on the other hand, have hours of nightly insomnia. Either I can't go to sleep at all, or if I do, I wake up and can't doze back off. My insomnia is always worse when we stay out of town.

One time we stayed in a motel in Charleston. I woke Russell up in the middle of the night to tell him to stop snoring, only to find out it was the person in the room beside us. It seems to me that snorers know no boundaries.

I don't snore, but Russell loves to tell our friends that I puff. He says I lie there and form my lips into what sounds like the first half of a snore, but then instead of exhaling, I hold onto the air a second or two, and out comes the puff. I've known only one puffer besides me in my whole life, and it was our minister. I never actually heard him puff (I would hope not), but his wife told the story one night at supper club and I believe her.

Russell came home one day so excited. He had seen an ad for Breathe Right strips, and a friend at work had told him the strips really worked. He bought a box, and that night he did not snore. For a long time the strips worked. But I think he became immune and as his system got stronger, the snoring returned periodically.

Snoring is a funny thing that affects us all in different ways. I have a friend who snores so badly that if she gets out of hand, her seven-year-old son comes into her room in the middle of the night and applies a Breathe Right strip to her nose.

Sometimes I would lie in bed at night wondering whether or

not Russell had a strip on. I would reach over and touch his nose, which almost caused him to have a heart attack. "Just checking," I would merrily say to the semi-conscious body next to me.

One night I couldn't stand the suspense any longer. I woke up Russell and asked him, "Honey, are you wearing your Breathe Right strip?"

"What?" he moaned. "A what? Yes, I am wearing one."

"I thought so," I beamed, "because I didn't hear you snoring."

That night, I saw a side of him that I had never seen before. Through clenched teeth he responded, "You woke me up to tell me that? Are you all right?"

"Sure, honey, I'm fine. Go on back to sleep," I said, yawning with contentment. I knew then he wouldn't be keeping me awake with his snoring. Relieved, I rolled over and puffed.

Where Do Broken Hearts Go? Home to Mama!

Riding down Interstate 95 near Savannah the other night, scanning the dial, I came across Delilah, the popular radio show host of "Love Someone Tonight." Now that's a job I'd like to have. Pretty cushy, huh? She's a successful DJ, giving advice, spinning a tune for that special someone, and keeping her fan club happy.

It's a pretty simple program. Listeners call up Delilah, lament their love loss, rejoice in a new or rekindled love interest, or just tell poignant anecdotes from their ordinary lives.

Russell and I were on our way to Florida that night, heading out for a seven-day cruise from Port Canaveral to the Eastern Caribbean. We were nearly one-third of the way through Georgia when I found her—Delilah, that is—with her sweet-but-sexy, oh-so-caring voice.

I decided to play along with her, sort of a "let's see if she's right" kind of game. A heartbroken young woman was the caller, and she spilled her guts immediately, saying she and her boyfriend weren't getting along. The caller described how her boyfriend had broken up with her and she missed him. She didn't know how she would live without him. She was just sick over the whole thing. Yadda, yadda, yadda.

Then came Delilah to the rescue. Initially, she just repeated the problem back to the caller. I call this The First Part.

Delilah wasted no time jumping to what I call The Second Part (the solution). *Snap to it, Missy*, I could hear her saying between the lines. Delilah was for sure going to set her straight and in record time (no pun intended).

So after the tired old saga of "I've lost my man, my heart, and worst of all, my brain," I began to see a pattern to this woman's misfortune. She said her boyfriend told her their relationship wasn't working out. He told her he needed (dare I say it?) *some space*. Not too original, but perhaps believable just the same.

Delilah pushed harder for more information. Little Susie Sadness confessed that her boyfriend drank too much. Delilah crooned, "Go on," her voice becoming deeper. Oops! The scorned woman had forgotten to mention that her boyfriend didn't have a job. To add insult to injury, the woman announced to the entire listening audience that her ex-sweetie pie was also living with his mama. *Well, there you have it.*

And yet, to my surprise, this woman simply wasn't giving up. She was desperate, betting against all odds that Delilah might wave her magic wand and fix the situation. Oh, no, not this time. Even Delilah couldn't change the facts. She suggested in a matter-of-fact way that the caller just might be better off without him. Gee, do you think? Duh!

This was when I decided Delilah is a dear. If it'd been me giving out the advice, I would have sworn at that fool. "Give it up, girl. The boy is a bum, a pure-tee loser. Why, it's as clear as the nose on your face!"

Then The Third Part (the music) came. It was time for Delilah to pick out a romantic melody, her signature "that's all folks, time's up" song.

Do you know what song Delilah picked that night? "Where Do Broken Hearts Go—Can They Find Their Way Home?" And I answered out loud, as we barreled down that open road with twinkling stars above, on a cool, clear, navy-blue night, "Sure, if they're living with Mama!"

For Whom the Bell Eventually Tolls: The Seven-Hour Wedding

Do you know what doesn't happen at a wedding when there's a bride and groom, but no minister? If you guessed "the ceremony," you're right. However, plenty of other activity took place on the day my friends Lisa and Rick were supposed to get married.

During their one-year engagement Lisa organized every detail, right down to the sandy beach where they would stand to recite their vows. She did everything right to prepare for the wedding: reserve the minister and wedding location (a coastal beach resort in South Carolina), hire a wedding coordinator, and select her bridal party well ahead of time. Everything was coming along well—maybe too well.

A friend at work teased her, "This is kind of scary. Things are so perfect only one week before your wedding. Don't you wonder if anything will go wrong?" Lisa was too cheerful to comment. She wasn't worried one bit.

The day of the wedding, Lisa, her mother, and her two attendants arrived at the resort early. Lisa sensed something was wrong the minute the wedding coordinator, Carol, walked up to her car. Sure enough, Carol blurted out, "The minister isn't here yet." Lisa froze, then yelled, "Well, find him!"

By now the guests were trickling in and walking down to the beach. Before long there were hushed whispers: *Why is the wedding delayed?* Carol told Lisa that things would be fine and not to worry. She had the ladies park the car in a shady spot where they wouldn't be seen. Lisa tried in vain to stay calm, sitting there for a full hour in the June heat, dressed in her formal gown and heels. It wasn't easy. She bit her nails. She fidgeted with her French twist. (It was no use —heavily-sprayed hairdos are like cotton candy, in that they both wilt and get sticky in high humidity.) Carol came by from time to time with a strained smile, telling jokes, being supportive, and giving updates on the absentee minister, who still hadn't answered his home or cell phone.

Others tried to help. A dear friend showed up with a welcome distraction: paper cups and wine. The nervous women drank the whole bottle while Carol rounded up a search party—three relatives who played detective. They followed orders and drove twenty miles to the pastor's town and back, hoping to find him, his wife, or his car. He was mysteriously, but clearly, missing.

Ever efficient, Carol began looking for a substitute. In the meantime, she arranged for the photographer to shoot pictures of Lisa and the three women. Eventually, she located an alternate minister and sent the ladies back to the house to freshen up. Sadly, the plan quickly soured when it was discovered that the original minister had the license.

At that point, Lisa lost it. What would they do? Call off the wedding? Run to South of the Border, a tourist complex famous for quickie weddings, some two hours away? Have a catered party for a hundred guests? Carol pleaded with Lisa to wait just a little longer. Grudgingly, she agreed.

As all talented wedding directors do, Carol kept things flowing smoothly. With the couple's permission, she started the reception early for the weary guests, who until now had been filling up on lemonade. The search for the pastor continued while inside the gala affair began, without the bride or groom. The guests danced to the DJ's music, enjoyed delicious food, and chatted while the photographer shot pictures of the groom and ushers, taking advantage of the beautiful sunset as a background.

Even Carol was losing patience now and was ready to give up when her cell phone rang. Come to find out, the minister had just checked his voice mail, and had somehow forgotten the wedding (but had remembered his golf game that afternoon). He apologized profusely and promised to rush. He'd be there in twenty minutes, after a quick stop by his house to get his robe, the marriage license, and the written ceremony. Carol thanked him over and over. She called Lisa, who bawled like a baby, then reapplied her makeup. After all, she was finally getting married.

Just then, Rick called Lisa and begged her, "Come on down!" He was inside the clubhouse and wanted to see her. She refused, saying if they'd waited this long, they could wait a little longer. She didn't want to break the tradition of the groom not seeing the bride on the day of the wedding. Now Rick was both disappointed with Lisa and annoyed at the minister. He said, "Honey, if I could just see your face."

Lisa spoke before thinking. "Well, just open your wallet to my picture." There was silence. Then they both laughed. She continued, "And anyway, if I can sit in a stuffy car in the June heat for five hours, you can darned well wait twenty minutes more to see me."

Finally the preacher arrived to loud cheers. There wasn't a dry eye on that sandy beach. Guests squeezed one another's hands and relieved friends winked. After the couple repeated their vows and turned to walk away, the minister scooted off. No doubt the man was embarrassed by his faux pas...or perhaps he planned to go home and study his Day-timer.

Lisa and Rick's was probably the longest wedding in history: seven hours from beginning to end, including a second reception after the ceremony. In years to come when they re-tell the events of their wedding day, it might sound to some like they're exaggerating. I assure you that it's all true.

Everything turned out fine in the end. And you know the best part? Despite their tumultuous beginning, the newly-wedded couple is now living happily ever after.

Did You Read <u>The</u> <u>Book</u>?

Well, it's that time again. Time for that sacred rite of passage—handing over the car keys to your family's newest driver.

It isn't like you don't know it's coming. In the great state of South Carolina, you have fifteen years to prepare, but that's not enough time. And anyway, who ever says, "Yes, she is mighty bright. She's saying complete sentences at eleven months. But what kind of a driver will she be?" Or, "His team won the soccer tournament. We are so proud. But will he be able to follow a road map? Turn on his blinkers? Back up straight?" You just never think about those things.

Plus, there's no warning. It's like one day, you pick your child up from school and she jumps in the car with glazed eyes and says, robot-like, "Remember, today is my birthday. I'm fifteen. Can we go to the Department of Motor Vehicles and get *the book?*" "*The book?*" you repeat.

Now, let me tell you about *the book.* When Russell drove over to get it, he stood in line for an hour while I sat melting in the July heat and humidity. (Never mind that I saw a friend, we chatted, and the time flew by. Don't tell Russell—otherwise, I wouldn't have had a reason to complain.) Russell wouldn't break into the line that was wrapped around the building for a simple request, "*The book*, please."

So then Katie studies the book and sure enough, she knows how to start the car, read the road signs, and push the gas pedal. I discovered a week later that, after a series of lessons from her father, she was still missing a couple of very important steps. The first clue came when I rode with her and, as we were leaving a parking space, she asked me, "Which direction do I turn the steering wheel?"

"Are you serious?" I asked. Then she put the car in reverse, began backing up, but didn't turn to look behind her. When I drilled her about this, she said her dad had never shown her that part.

By some miracle, we got home unscathed. Katie drove into our garage, which usually yields an equal eight feet on each side between the vehicle and the wall. The car ended up with one foot of space on the left and fifteen feet of space on the right.

I asked Katie exactly where she and her father had practiced. Come to find out they just drove around Waccamaw High School one Sunday afternoon. No other cars or traffic, and it would seem, no parking, no backing up, and no three-point turns. Heck, sounds like she just practiced gliding, not driving.

Katie walked back to her bedroom, and I stood in the garage, experiencing déjà vu. I thought back to our other daughter Kelly's early driving days. On one of Kelly's first solo trips, she ran down a mailbox in our subdivision on prom night, before the prom even began. She was in full makeup, complete with light blue eyeshadow and big hair. All the primping in the world didn't make it any easier for her to tell me the bad news. I must say her embarrassed, "Mama, I'm sorry, but I wrecked the car, sort of," clashed with her grown-up, confident appearance. She convinced me to go explain the situation to our neighbor Carl (whose mailbox it was), and I felt sorry for her, so I did.

He wasn't mad. I guess Carl had been through a similar experience in the past with his teenage son. He just looked at me, paused, then smiled slyly, saying, "Did she read *the book?*"

Pile High!
The Importance of
Being Ordered

My life is ordered by piles. Or maybe I should say, my life is organized—or disorganized as the case may be—by piles. You know, like a pile of this and a pile of that.

Clutter control and clutter patrol are not in my vocabulary. (This was not always true, but that was many moons ago, before having babies, a pack-rat husband, and a job.) I envy those people who stay organized. You know the type. They have piles too, but with a method to their madness. Theirs are hidden away in dresser drawers and cabinets, shelves and closets.

A friend once told me, "When you clean out your closet, make three piles. One is for clothes you want to give away, one's for clothes you haven't worn in a year, and one is for clothes you do wear." So I did that, and you know what? Those piles just sat there! After staring at the sorted clothing for weeks, I eventually got rid of most of it. Some items made their way back into the closet on hangers, and a few are still in a pile in the back corner. Okay, so it's also hard for me to make decisions.

If I was ever dropped off on a deserted island (yes, something Russell threatens to do), I wouldn't take along food and water, a favorite book, walking shoes, or a writing journal. Instead, I would choose a pile—make that several piles—from my home. In fact, that's one reason I don't hire a cleaning service. Even though I'm not organized, I have my favorite pile and no one is allowed to touch it. Plus, I know I would suffer from pile withdrawal when the cleaners got through.

As I write this, I spot a pile of receipts, a pile of sticky-notes, a pile of photos, a pile of magazines, a pile of bills, a pile of mail, a pile of articles, and a pile of I'm-not-sure-what-it-is.

Car trips are impossible because I usually transport my piles with me. One big problem is by the time I get all settled in the car and ready for the trek to my parents' home, for instance, three hours away, there is no room left for me. I always end up with four square inches of room for my feet, and I have to angle myself *just so*.

By the time I lay out my notebook, cutesy mall-shop bag with those darling paper handles, cloth bag from Estée Lauder, sack of snack food, my pocketbook, and all my CDs and tapes, I'm left with no seat! Don't tell me to stick it all in my trunk, either. I've tried that and I can't get two miles before I pull over, pop the lid, and start grabbing from those piles.

After three or four stops to retrieve whatever, whenever, wherever, I realize it's hopeless to be pileless.

Welcome to My Home, and Watch Your Step

If we ever have a national disaster, you might not want to come to my house to camp out. For one thing, I am a compulsive kitchen minimalist, so mealtime might involve sparse rations. You can usually find one shriveled carrot, two sprouted potatoes, or maybe a tablespoon of peanut butter in the kitchen, but certainly not enough to fill a plate. It's a bad habit I've gotten into and it's a true dilemma.

On the one hand, there *is* food in the house. On the other hand, it might not be edible. This drives my daughter Kelly crazy—or so she says. I always spot a gleam in her eye when, after a long trip here from Raleigh, she puts her suitcase in the bedroom, primps in the bathroom mirror for a few minutes, and then goes straight to the refrigerator and cleans it out. Next she runs sudsy dishwater in the sink. Then the Tupperware goes flying, and the garbage can fills up quickly. It's a routine I've come to expect.

For another thing, the sanitation rating here might not get a grade of "A." Once when Katie was fourteen, she had a friend over for dinner. Afterward, Jessica picked up the broom and began sweeping my kitchen. "I just can't stand it any longer," she told Katie, with tear-filled eyes. Her mother still doesn't believe this, since she's never seen her child hold a broom. In my defense, things do get cleaner the higher up you go. The ceiling, for instance, is spotless.

Then there is the matter of grounds. I think I know where the term "grounds for divorce" comes from—unsuspecting spouses who choke on menacing black flecks in their glasses of iced tea. Am I the only one who has this problem with bursting tea bags? The process seems simple. I boil the bags and water, then let the pot steep for five minutes. Next I throw away the bags and pour the tea into the pitcher. I add sugar and stir. Easy enough, so far. Suddenly I spot tiny black grounds floating to the top. I strain the tea as best I can —after all, I hate to waste—and fill up the glasses. Sometimes this works and sometimes it doesn't. The dilemma is especially embarrassing when we have company over. Russell is usually the one to notice first. His special "tea grounds-cough" is my cue to throw out the remaining tea in the pitcher.

I've always said if my beds are made up, I feel like my house is clean...or should I say clean enough? If you came to visit, you would get a clean, made bed, not to mention a warm welcome.

There are welcome signs all over my house and even in the yard. Russell says he hopes we're never burglarized because it would be hard to prove in court that anyone had trespassed, what with all those welcome signs. We have cross-stitched signs, ceramic signs, découpaged signs, banners, and flags.

Hey, what can I say? So what if my house isn't the cleanest one on the block and the food choices are sparse. With a warm welcome and a cozy place to sleep, two out of four isn't bad!

Secret Service Men...So Cool They Make Me Drool

It has been fascinating thus far observing President George W. Bush in office. Okay, let me rephrase that: It has been fascinating observing President George W. Bush in office surrounded by his secret service men. Where do these guys come from? They are so purrrrrrrrrrfect!

In an effort to learn more about this specialized field, I perused the Internet. I often equate secret service men with James Bond, but here are the facts: They must be U.S. citizens and between the ages of twenty-one and thirty-seven at the time of appointment. Their vision can be no worse than 20/60 (uncorrected) in each eye and must be correctable to 20/20. They must have a bachelor's degree from an accredited college or university or a minimum of three years' experience, of which two years must be in criminal investigation.

Although I didn't read that good looks are a prerequisite for the job, you and I know they are. Come on, now. These hunky males are drop-dead gorgeous, sort of like Mr. Ivy League, Chippendale-model, GQ, Rhodes Scholar, Perfect-10, and Adonis all rolled into one. They don't sweat, don't frown, don't smile either, don't crouch over, do move gracefully, don't lose their cool, and don't cuss. Wait a minute, did I say don't cuss? I don't believe they ever talk.

I wonder just where these men come from. Is some proud mama back home beaming at that front-page picture and telling all her friends, "Yes, Latricia, he was always a knockout. Men feared him and fish hated him. Oh yes, it's true. He was president of the student council. Oh, and did I mention captain of the basketball team? And valedictorian?"

Now, I realize that many mothers secretly hope their daughters will grow up and marry doctors, lawyers, or at the very least, responsible, dependable, productive members of society. But I say, why not hope she will marry a secret service man? Now that's a lofty goal!

You have to admit, these guys would learn an awful lot hanging around the White House, what with making sure the President is safe, comfortable, and given the freedom to move about. They get to see the world and travel to exotic places, so they'd make great conversationalists. And finally, any man in this elite force is going to be so photogenic, you know he would only add to the perfect family portrait one day.

The Web site I researched also had a list of the agents' required training. My eyes were indeed opened. I can see what fine husbands these men would make in terms of resourcefulness, perception, and ingenuity.

The list of mandatory educational programs for new hires didn't have explanations, so I left that part up to my imagination. Here is what I envisioned that the maybe-too-perfect, ready-for-anything secret agent would say to his pretty-much-normal wife:

On extensive physical fitness and conditioning: "Now, darling, I don't care how big your wedding dress and crinoline are, I am too going to carry you over the threshold on our honeymoon. It's a tradition."

Rules of evidence: "Honey, the chicken seems burnt. Your mother was the one who cooked the chicken. Therefore, my mother-in-law burnt the chicken."

Emergency medicine: "These nine months have sure flown by. If the doctor is away playing golf, you can count on me to deliver little junior here."

Comprehensive courses in protection: While hiking on a vacation: "Don't worry, sweetie, I know we're 2,000 feet above sea level with no park ranger for miles around, but I promise that I'll defend us against that grizzly bear."

Surveillance techniques: "So dear, I was just wondering. When are you going to wear that $200 dress with the tags still attached, hidden in the back of the closet?"

Protective and defensive driving measures: "Sit back and relax, everybody. No problem. I'll get us through this fourth of July bumper-to-bumper traffic in plenty of time to catch Myrtle Beach's Carolina Opry, even if it does start in five minutes."

Use of scientific devices: "Well, Ms. Santa Claus, what should I do now? If I install all fourteen strands of bulbs you've given me to decorate the Christmas tree, I'm going to overload the circuits."

Yeah, I think we ought to keep an eye on these interesting fellows. If you're like me and love to play matchmaker, send this column to your favorite single woman friend. There could be some guy on Presidential guard duty dreaming about a home-cooked meal and a little dinner conversation right about now. Hey, with all of his specialized skills, maybe he could fly over and parachute onto her patio tonight.

Like I said, it has been fascinating so far...

Those Aren't My Shoes!
They're Too Clean

There is one piece of advice I have had to learn the hard way: Never lend your old, beat-up shoes to your best friend. You may never see them again. Also, never lend this person a sifter or, say, a bathing suit. Case in point:

By mistake, I left a pair of white canvas Keds in Becky's car a couple of years ago and she just brought back the left one yesterday. She said that was because she hadn't seen the bottom of her car in all that time. When I asked her about the other shoe, she didn't have a clue. After several weeks I threw out the one she returned (what good was one sneaker?!), only to have her deliver the mate many months later.

She's never been able to explain how she lost the sifter I lent her, which belonged to my great-grandmother. Now, excuse me, but how does someone lose a ten-by-six-inch metal sifter with a handle and mesh screen? I could see losing a spool of thread, a measuring spoon, or cup of sugar (I'm only trying to make a point here), but a sifter? Come on!

I can just hear Becky saying, "Well, I guess I accidentally threw it away right after I baked the twelve-layer cake. I'm also missing the eight-by-eleven-inch pan and the beaters and bowl; do you think a cake robber came in when I wasn't looking?"

Because Becky and I are old friends and share many common interests, we often exchange recipes and necessary ingredients we're short on. She once borrowed my crockpot to cook meatballs, along with the recipe and some chili powder. Surprisingly, she brought these items back one week later.

I've appreciated all the items Becky did return over the years. I have missed all those items Becky has lost over the years. I'm still dumbfounded as to why and how she returned one Ked...then the match, months later.

Then last week we rode to the gym in Becky's car. She was at my house and had no gym clothes or shoes with her, so I lent her mine. This was the same day I spotted the bathing suit I had lent her in the trunk of her car, wrapped in a plastic bag, growing a beautiful hue of turquoise mold.

I'd forgotten about lending her the clothes and shoes until this evening, when she stopped by and had on some vaguely familiar-looking Reeboks. I decided they couldn't be mine because mine were sandy, scuffed, and old. These were clean, white, and in terrific shape. I asked her, "Whose shoes are those?" "Yours," she replied, embarrassed. We actually argued over it. "They aren't mine. They're too clean. Did you wash them?" I probed, to which she answered, "They are too, and I did not wash them."

Okay, I believe you, Becky, but just let me say this: Sifters or sneakers, crockpots or chili powder, never a borrower or lender be. Just gimme my stuff, half or whole, and you'll see a smiling me.

chapter 5

Fighting Technology and Other Culprits

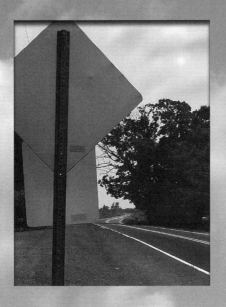

I'm Seeing Red,
But I'm Not Feeling Blue

I'm seeing red…but I'm not feeling blue, even though darned near everything I've bought lately has been red. It all began over a year ago when I sponge-painted my entryway red—more of a deep cranberry, but to the average observer, red. Then I redid my bedroom walls in pale celery (don't you love naming colors in food-themes?) with complementary shades of red. I chose a pomegranate-colored Ralph Lauren floral comforter with Christmas-berry undertones for accessories: bed skirt, pillows, candles, picture frames, etc.

Surrounded by all this red, I noticed a decidedly happier me. As time went on, I found myself drifting toward other red objects, such as china, linens, flowers, even reddish highlights for my hair. Shoot, I even bought a red mini-flashlight for my key chain, then later a red heart. (In fact, I collect red hearts, and my favorite piece of jewelry is a gold charm bracelet with gold and red hearts.)

Most experts agree that red is an electrifying, anxiety-producing color, but I have found just the opposite to be true. Red calms me. Go figure. Maybe it's because I'm already hyper as all-get-out on any given day and the red kind of levels out the playing field. When I was a child and anyone would ask, "What's your favorite color?" I always said, "Blue." I'm not sure that was the case but it was a safe answer and no one made fun of me with that reply—even though I thought red, yellow, and orange were much prettier. I think now that it takes a bold person to appreciate such a bold color.

And for sure, I've gotten bolder over the years. I see that every major purchase I've made in the last few months has been in red.

Case in point: Along about June, Russell and I bought a new SUV, a Kia Sportage, and it's red. It would have been a good-looking enough vehicle in forest-green or white—I've seen them both and like them. But red is so me! I scoot around town feeling like the little engine that could. No, it doesn't go real fast and it's not all that sleek, but it's the color that does it for me.

Maybe it's merely a coincidence that Katie began attending the University of South Carolina this past fall and their school colors are garnet and black, but I don't know. I do know how tickled I felt when we first went to the bookstore. Everything was red! Pencils, pens, pads of paper, banners, stickers, T-shirts, sweatshirts, and of course, stadium seats.

If they'd sold furniture, that would have been even better. I'd been searching for a new living room suite for well over a year and couldn't find quite the right color. Yes, I secretly hoped to find something in red, but never dreamed I would find anything that wasn't too ostentatious, glitzy, or heaven forbid, rust-looking.

I drove from Charleston to Wilmington and back and only saw one red sofa that I'd consider, and it was leather. However, its price tag had me seeing red; I think it cost $3850. So I kept looking.

Then one day my friend Debbie and I were piddling around in Myrtle Beach. I left a parking lot, looked straight ahead, and saw a furniture store that I remembered was new in the area. "Will you run in there with me," I asked Debbie, "just for fun?" She agreed and off we went. We walked inside, and there it was smack dab at the front door entrance—the clearest-red and most elegantly-styled sofa and matching chair I'd ever seen. "That's it!" I squealed. Both pieces were oversized with a denim-like texture. I sunk down into the chair and nearly fell asleep, it was so comfy. I made a note of the size, price, and delivery information, then promised the clerk I'd return with Russell later in the week.

That Sunday after church Russell and I visited the store, and he immediately gave me a thumb's up, claiming the chair was "his" before we even got it home. He especially liked the size since he is a big guy at six-foot-two.

Funny thing was that the salesman told me they were having a private sale for their special, valued customers, and he'd like to offer it to me. I'm not sure, but he seemed to be whispering. *How wonderful*, I thought. He looked around, then quickly handed me a folded flyer on which he'd scribbled a personal note. I read it immediately, surprised to find the note was addressed to someone else, not me—but the customer's last name was unusual, and I was pretty sure it was one of my friend's. I told Greg about the mistake and he quickly scribbled out her name, inserted mine, and handed the paper back to me. (So much for my feeling special.) Flash forward a week later to where we did indeed buy the sofa and chair, and had it delivered the day before we left for our cruise—a one-week vacation to the Caribbean.

Several times during our trip I told Russell how I couldn't wait to see our new furniture when we got back home. Other passengers mentioned feeling homesick—missing a puppy or a child, some even said spouses. I chimed right in and told everyone I missed my sofa, and I did.

On the drive back from Florida we stopped to have dinner at the Seewee Restaurant in Awendaw. Who did I run into, but the same friend whose name was written on the advertising flyer at the furniture store! Jean and I attend the same church, are both in supper club, and our friendship spans well over fifteen years. She and her husband along with his brother and wife had just returned from a Citadel game and were walking out the door as we walked in.

I couldn't wait to tell her the sofa story. Sure 'nuff! She not only liked the exact same sofa, she bought the entire set: sofa, loveseat, chair, and ottoman. We laughed to think of the chances. Later, at our supper club get-together, we told everyone about our furniture purchase. Emma Ruth, who swore she'd considered buying a red sofa for years, promised to go have a look at the store. I suggested Sara Dee do the same, and Sherry said she might too. If we keep this up, we'll be known as the Red Sofa Society.

I must be a magnet for red, because now it seems to be finding me instead of vice-versa. Last weekend we took a day trip to Charleston and on the way home, ran in Victoria's Secrets in Mt. Pleasant. Katie and I were just browsing. We didn't plan to buy anything, but as often happens, the SALE sign lured us in. Then I spotted them: gorgeous 100% cotton red pajamas laying on a table, tied with an elegant red ribbon. There was one medium in the entire store and they fit me like Cinderella's glass slipper. I bought the PJs and have hardly taken them off since.

It's getting kind of kooky around here, my being lost in a sea of red. Last night Russell stood in the den and called out my name, saying, "Ann, where are you?"

I looked right at him and said, "Silly, I'm right here." I could see why he was confused—there was nothing but a patch of red (even red slippers) sitting on a cloud of red (the oversized chair). He said that if it hadn't been for my smiling pink face, he never would have found me.

Voice Mail? Voice Misery? Press, Repeat, and Hold

D° you know what the leading cause of anxiety for the average American is today? It's not high taxes or the unstable economy. It's not insurance woes or health concerns. It's not our education system or our political leadership. It's—are you ready?—voice mail, or what I prefer to call "Voice Misery."

We Americans have become so high-tech—so high-optic fiber connected, so wireless-based, so cable-ready—that no one, I repeat, no one, can reach anyone anymore. The other day I called a popular tourist resort, and by the time I hung up, I'd written down an entire legal pad of instructions. All the while, I never did talk to a real person. The conversation (or the lack thereof, because conversation requires both individuals speak and listen) went like this:

"If you know your party's extension, you may dial it at any time." I knew the extension, but I was curious, so I kept listening. "If the party's last name begins with A, dial 1. B, dial 2."

What party? I wasn't invited to a party. Next, the Voice Misery lady told me that if I wanted to bypass this recording, I could press zero for the next available operator (who would be free to assist me sometime within the next ten minutes to five hours). Otherwise, the main menu would be repeated. Do what?

Then the voice asked me to punch in the first three digits of my last name. Why? I wanted to punch something, but it wasn't the phone's keypad.

Then the voice instructed that if I needed to be transferred to Customer Service, I should dial one number, if I wanted Technical Assistance, dial another, and if I wanted to Scream, press a third number (not really, but it sounded good). After twenty minutes of this, I hung up and wandered about my office, traumatized.

I got a cup of coffee, did a few stretching exercises, and took a restroom break. *Okay, I can handle this,* I thought. I took a nice, deep breath, settled into my chair, and decided to try one more time.

Hey, I'd done this before, so each step got easier. I dialed one, then four. Next I hit five-two-five-four. Oh, yeah, I was on a roll. I pushed seven. Then I waited. Nothing.

I realized I could likely stop playing this numbers game simply by pressing zero. At least then I would hear a human voice. I dialed zero, elated at the thought of talking to a real person...

After a few seconds I heard that horrible Voice Misery lady's voice: "I'm sorry. The party you are calling does not wish to speak to you. If you need further assistance, please hang up and dial the operator."

I needed assistance all right, but in the form of Extra-Strength Tylenol. Dialing zero once more, I reached the operator and asked her if she could *puhlllllllease* send me written instructions on voice mail or Voice Misery.

She answered in a polite, robotic voice, "I'm sorry. Voice mail or Voice Misery, either way you look at it, we're not allowed to assist you. You are on a solitary mission, same as everyone else. However, if you'd like my supervisor's voice mail, please hang up and dial..."

Carrying Forward the Fight Against Mold

Katie is home for the summer from Governor's School. Having her here has been fun most of the time and challenging at other times. Some things never change. She hated housework before she left home, and I'd guess she hates it even more now.

I wondered why the last time Katie cleaned her bathroom—the job she detests the most—she was able to finish in less than thirty seconds. Apparently, she conveniently overlooked the mold hidden around the bathtub faucet and drain. We had houseguests coming, and Katie's credo is that guests' visits are the only reason we should "deep clean" the house.

Thinking back, I realize that during the time I searched for the Soft Gel, which she swore was missing, she'd finished. I walked in, cleaner in hand, and she said, "Never mind, I'm through." I was in a hurry and didn't push the point. I didn't even make my usual drill sergeant inspection (which I'm famous for). I think I was preoccupied being a domestic goddess that day, baking brownies or mopping the kitchen floor. Don't laugh, I do those things about twice a year.

A few days later I was working on the computer when Katie walked up to me, waved a ten-by-fourteen-inch clear package, and asked, "Mom, who is this new shower curtain for?" (It was actually a shower curtain liner.) "You," I replied. "It's for your bathroom." Then she asked me why I bought it, as there was nothing wrong with her present one. "Oh, yeah? Follow me," I commanded.

We walked down the hall together, into her bathroom. Throwing back the hanging plastic, I pointed. "Just look!" I yelled, sounding like Cruella DeVille. (I love drama and that felt darned good.) I searched her face for signs of understanding. She just shrugged. "So what is it?" she asked. "Mold!" I said. Those old Lowcountry menaces—mold and mildew—had once again managed to sneak up on us, clinging to our shower curtain liner for their very lives. The old shower curtain itself was perfectly fine, thanks to the liner (not so fine) that protected it. Let me explain:

Katie and I redecorated her bathroom a year ago. We (okay, I admit it, actually Russell) painted the walls a darling lilac color. I stress the word lilac, because Russell asked me at the time why I wanted to paint the bathroom purple. "It's not purple," I replied. Of course, since then, everyone who sees the room says, "Oh, I just love that purple." This drives me crazy. We also replaced the tarnished brass cabinet knobs. Oh sure, I tried Brasso first, but the salt air had eaten away two layers too many of brass. Next, Katie and I went shopping and found an adorable combed-cotton, loopy lilac rug and commode cover to match. That rug feels soooooooooo good on your bare feet. We then located a precious little shadowbox with a tassel inside to hang on the wall. What the significance of that tassel was, I don't know, but it had a touch of lilac, so why did I care?

Finally, we discovered the perfect shower curtain with swirls of lilac and sage green, kind of foresty-looking. One problem though: That shower curtain cost more than the original sink, tub, and toilet put together. Then it hit me. It was actually going to get wet! Then here come the mold and mildew, I realized. I almost sat down and cried while paying the clerk.

The obvious solution (and the cheapest purchase of all) ended up being a $2.95 disposable liner that would, in a short time, grow mold. And not just any mold, mind you. In just a few short months, we got iridescent mold, with swirled streaks of pink, blue, black, and sometimes even lilac. Hey, at least it's color-coordinated. And if you take a few steps back and close one eye, it looks like a Monet painting. At least I solved the mold problem without spending a fortune. And they say blondes aren't smart!

Colorful Solutions to Purse Snatching

What's up with all this purse snatching that I've been reading about in the papers lately? I mean, come on. How low can you go? Purse snatching is the pits!

I believe a woman's purse is her very essence. It's as much a part of her as, say, her frosted hair. And anyway, why would anyone else want what's inside? Take my purse, for instance (no pun intended). Inside you'll find used Kleenex, half-melted lipstick, a wide-tooth comb, my checkbook (balance zero), my wallet (balance also zero), candy wrappers, leaky ballpoint pens, paper clips, and paper scraps with lipstick blots. Not interesting.

I get furious whenever I read about a purse snatching, especially when the victim is an innocent little old lady. I can just picture this sweetheart shelling butterbeans all morning, baking biscuits, and cooking up a pot roast to serve her family at noon. Afterwards, it's off to the mall to buy some support hose. Next thing you know, *bam!* When she steps out of her car, some thug tries to grab her purse. Well, I sure don't advocate violence. In fact, I abhor it. But I do believe in self-defense.

Truth is, if she had that purse loaded just right, it would become an effective weapon. When the would-be robber approached, she could spin that thing over her shoulder, getting up some momentum, and then release the full weight at his thick skull. Problem solved. Out he'd go, like a light.

Here's another thought: You know how they put red dye in all the money packs at the bank? Why not sell purses equipped with a small vial of purple dye that activates when someone pulls on the strap? Let the little creep go ten feet down the road with your stolen purse and have the whole thing explode in his face. Of course, your twenty-five-dollar tube of lipstick would be ruined by the time the police returned the purse to you, but that sacrifice would be a small one if it stopped the thief from stealing again.

Another solution would be to re-introduce those handy fanny-packs that were popular in the '80s. It'd be pretty tough for a criminal to unsnap the buckle that connects the wallet to the strap. Heck, I had trouble unlocking mine.

Oh, my daughters hated those things with a passion. I remember one trip we made to Disney World about ten years ago. I spent most of the trip wandering around the park alone because Kelly and Katie were too embarrassed to be seen with me. "Oh *Mommmmm*, why do you *have* to carry that hideous-looking thing?" they whined. They would hide it at night when we got back to the motel, hoping I'd never find it, but I always did. Of course, Russell stayed pretty close to me that trip because the fanny pack held the money, and I shelled out the cash for the meals.

Surely there is a simple and effective solution that could put an end to purse snatching, and at the same time, teach the evil-doer the difference between right and wrong. It makes me wonder if these desperate criminals ever went to kindergarten, where they surely would have learned self-control and common courtesy.

Never grab what is not yours. Remember that rule? Come to think of it, living that one motto alone could take a huge bite out of crime, political corruption, and domestic abuse. Maybe we ought to offer public kindergarten in schools and colleges for those people who never went in the first place or somehow forgot the basic rules of life. They'd get to learn/relearn manners, kindness, and honesty. Whaddya say?

You Don't Smell Swell, and You're Giving Me a Headache

The other night I was talking to my good friend Betsy Harper, a very talented portrait artist here in Pawleys Island. We were discussing how much we enjoy fruit-scented lotions and soaps, oils and candles, perfumes and body sprays. Thanks to all the new bath and beauty shops everywhere, there is something for everyone.

Only problem I see is when I run out of, say, the kiwi lotion, I still have three bars of kiwi soap. I can never even it up. Do I return to the specialty store and buy more kiwi lotion? Survey says, "No!" So now I have strawberry soap, peach lotion, apple body spray, and blueberry perfume. It's enough to make me feel like a walking fruit basket. (Russell prefers to call me a "fruitcake" though.) In fact, if you'd just add a little whipped cream and pound cake to my medicine cabinet, you'd have enough dessert to last three years.

If fruit-scented products aren't your thing, there's always cosmetics created with essential oils and fragrant herbs, including musk, eucalyptus, almond, camphor, cinnamon, lavender, and mint. No wonder so many people have sinus problems. It's not the pollen or the rye grass. It's the super-pungent smells. Go to any show or performance, and at least one woman (yes, nine times out of ten it's a woman, I admit it) will be enveloped in perfume fumes. And guess what, she always sits in front of me—or worse yet, right beside me. Gag me! I want to say, "Listen here, dear. You don't smell swell, and you're giving me a headache."

Several months back, I picked up some body spray for Katie. She'd been sick, and when I went to get her prescription, I stopped by the good-smelling rack and found her a surcie. (That's what my family calls a surprise gift.) You know what, she's been using this stuff as body spray for a year. The other night I was getting ready to spray some on me and realized the label said "linen spray." Oops!

Now I've heard it all. Not only do we spray our bodies, use air fresheners, apply carpet sanitizers, and rub on clothes enhancers, we also mist our darn pillows. I don't think that's what they had in mind when the song, "Sweet Dreams, Baby" was written.

I wonder what's next for our aroma-obsessed nation. I have to tell you, I think it's going to get worse before it gets better. Here's an example: I recently noticed a bizarre novelty item: a fruit-scented pen. I'm sorry, but when I'm writing out my bills, I don't care a flip about smelling strawberries. Perhaps the next new item the stationery supply stores will stock is money-scented pens. Now, that might make sense, no pun intended.

I was at my parents' house recently. I noticed that my mother had a can of no-smell neutralizing spray in the bathroom. I'd never heard of such a thing, but I think the people who created it might be onto something. Since we are all so anxious to eliminate obnoxious odors like smoke, pollution, and mold and mildew, I suppose neutralizing is the way to go.

Actually, I believe I'll buy a trial-size container of the no-smell stuff to keep in my purse. Then the next time I sit down beside a heavily perfumed woman, I can reach in my bag and neutralize her pesky aroma. What a great pollution solution!

Cars Versus UOFs
(Unidentified Ongoing Fiascos)

I've heard there are people who drive their cars for one purpose and one purpose only: to get to where they are going. I say those people are boring. I get a lot more creative than that when I drive. I once took a cake decorating class at Horry Georgetown Tech. I remember the night well. It was rainy and dark, and the parking lot was full of potholes. Water was standing fairly deep in places, and I never noticed the orange traffic cone until after I'd driven over it. Apparently my car just sucked the cone up. It landed upright, square under the tire. What I did notice was the screeching, agonized sound my car began to make. The bad thing was, I had to find a parking place. What does everyone do when it rains? Park at the front of the building. So I had to go around back, and this gave the cone plenty of time to get really stuck. I don't remember how my cake turned out that evening, but I do remember the sweetheart of a guy who wrestled the two-foot menace free. He didn't even ask me how it happened, bless his heart.

Another time I was out driving and stopped at a Christmas tree farm. I decided to come back later when Russell could help me make a decision, and okay, I'll admit it, help me load the twenty-pound fraser fir, since I couldn't even lift it off the ground. As I was leaving the parking lot, a huge piece of heavy, clear plastic wrap flew off a tree and literally melted itself to my muffler. The smell! The absurdity! The atrocity! It was years before my car got back to normal.

Then, when I was on my way to church one Sunday morning, I rolled right over a shiny metal object. I heard the air whzzzzzzz out of my tires. I stopped and borrowed a friend's phone to call Russell. I don't know how many times he asked me how I managed to drive right over a pair of needle-nose pliers.

But wait, there's more. There was the used Chevette we bought about eighteen years ago. Within a month it had a burned-out clutch and a broken gas gauge. My father prides himself on keeping a full tank of gas, and it just so happened I ran out of gas right in front of his shoe store. He walked out to the car with me, looked at the front dash, and said, "Well, no wonder! You're sitting on empty." I didn't dare tell him the gauge was broken.

Not only do I have bad luck when driving, Russell will be the first to tell you I'm a terrible navigator as well. (Of course, that's *his* opinion.) We get along pretty well most days, but don't put us in a car together on a long trip. He doesn't believe in maps, and usually I don't have one, it's outdated, or I can't follow it. One on-going argument we have is over the speed limit. He says when the speed limit on the highway changes from, say, forty-five to fifty-five, you can't increase your speed until you've passed the sign. I say that is ridiculous. The minute my eyes focus on the new number (and oft times I've memorized it anyway), I say go for it. Also, Russell won't drive one mile over the speed limit. I argue, "They give you five miles!" He counters, "They don't give you anything." Okay, but figure this out: Ask Russell how many speeding tickets he has had (one) and how many I've had (none). So what if I backed into a car years ago when I was leaving a restaurant, and so what if I ran into a car at a drawbridge when the light turned yellow, and so what if...never mind. You get the picture. (Doesn't everyone drive over the concrete bumper stopper in parking lots at least once in their lifetime?)

After I had had a recent chiropractic adjustment, Russell, Katie, and I went out to dinner. As we were leaving, I watched in horror as Russell drove the car off the curb. As the right front tire went over a ten-inch drop-off, I grabbed my neck with both hands and yelled, "Oh no, there goes my alignment." Because Russell was watching me (with a puzzled expression) instead of the road, he not only hit that curb but another one as well. Hysterical laughter overcame me. This continued as he drove to Harris Teeter. We got out and shopped while I dabbed tears from my reddened, swollen face, still laughing. Then it finally hit Russell. He stopped right there in front of the black-eyed peas and asked, "What'd you say about your fifty-dollar spinal alignment? How about the alignment of our $20,000 car?" Sounds just like something he'd say, huh?

Car Talk
(The Joy of Tune-Ups)

Few things get me riled like a car tune-up. Since it takes a week or so from the time you call the shop until your appointment (they are *so busy* they tell you), just the thought of it gives me plenty of time to say, develop high blood pressure or have nightmares.

On the dreaded day of the appointment (circled in red on my calendar) this is what happens: First of all, the lobby where you wait is a mecca for people watchers. You see every type of person on the planet earth—it's a sampling of what all is really *out there*. Most times, everyone is sitting on cracked imitation-leather, back-breaking chairs. Invariably, the TV is blaring and there is a disgusting talk show going on at the loudest volume. Someone is usually whining to the host about how her mother's boyfriend stole her cousin's patent on a rocky marriage relift. The coffee is always—and I mean *always*—cold, and thick as well. Oh, and they never have cream and sugar. They do have packets of that dry, powdery hardened stuff lined up beside little red sticks that are sharp enough to poke your eye out.

Keeping all this in mind, I usually take four or five books to read, my writer's journal, a sketchbook, and my bank statement to balance my checking account—anything to keep me busy and make the time fly by (which it never does).

The last time I got my Buick tuned up at the car dealership where I bought the car, a very serious ordeal ensued. A four-to-five-hour wait is the norm. I had been sitting there for only about two hours when this worried-looking man came into the lobby, carrying a clipboard and wearing a perfectly-starched blue uniform with absolutely no grease on it.

"Miz Ippoc," he announced. They always say my name wrong.

I corrected him, "I-pock." (Long I—rhymes with lock.)

"Who?" he said and continued. "You may want to step over here."

Uh-oh. *Step over here.* I knew that couldn't be good.

He whispered, "I've got some bad news."

At that moment, my head began to swim and my knees got weak. I braced myself for the worst. "Please go ahead," I said cautiously.

"You see, Miz Ippoc, we've got a big problem with your vehicle. The double piston is coming off the steering python, and the quadruple by-hangar is taking a jolt off the T11 412 carburetor. I'm going to level with you, it's real bad."

"What are you saying? How much will that cost?" I asked.

"It's hard to guess. We are going to need to keep it overnight for observation."

"Are you serious?" I yelled.

"Please, keep your voice down. You'll upset the others."

"Tell you what," I told him, "why don't you fly in a team of surgeons from Johns Hopkins to look at it, and at the same time they can repair all the bones in you I am about to break."

"Or," he continued, "we could just put in a quart of oil and let you think about it overnight."

I replied, "Yeah, right. Maybe I need a second opinion anyway."

He handed me the keys, and I gathered my things. As I was walking out the door I overheard the same mechanic walk up and announce, "Miz Carter, you might want to step over here…"

Having One of Those Days?

It's like when you go to the grocery store and there's only one gallon of one-percent milk left (but lots of two-percent, whole milk, and heavy cream), and the expiration date of the one-percent is the date on your watch. Do you buy the good-for-you milk and drink it real fast so it won't spoil? Or do you buy the high-cholesterol milk and take your time drinking it so the fat won't build up in your body so quickly?

So then you make your choice and proceed to the checkout. The checker asks you do you want plastic or paper. In other words, do you want plastic so the bags can grow into one humongous ball in your storage closet, where they might eventually touch the water heater and melt all over it? Or do you want paper so you can accumulate over 500 bags in a month, wedged between the clothes dryer and the wall where they might catch on fire? You tell the checker, through clenched teeth, just to decide for you. One more decision that day and you might go over the edge. Giving you a frightened look, she slips the milk into a plastic bag and with a tilt of her head and an arched eyebrow, signals the manager to keep an eye on you just in case.

Then you walk to your car with a buggy that makes those terrible headache-inducing noises (*kabuda, kabuda*) going over the asphalt bumps. (Do they ever align buggies?) You tie the plastic bag holding the milk, so that if the container turns over, the spillage will stay in the bag. You place the bags in your trunk and off you drive. You pull into your garage, open your trunk—and guess what? The plastic bag holding the milk is still tied in a knot, but the carton turned over and is lying on its side. It must have flipped a couple of times, because some of the milk is still in the container, but some of it has indeed leaked into the trunk. You carry the milk inside and, for the life of you, you cannot untie the knot. You also can't find your scissors. So you pull and you pull until your fingers are red and raw. Giving up, you walk out to the car. You sop up the milk from the carpet of the trunk as best you can, go back inside, and put the other groceries away. Then you decide to drive to the car wash to use the heavy-duty mounted vacuum cleaner (because you figured the smell would sour and ruin the carpet) only to find the car wash closed, and a homemade sign posted that reads, *Left early. Gone for groceries. Check back tomorrow.*

A New Set of Eyes

I have been wearing contacts for almost two years now. Before I even considered this, my daughter, who is squeamish about some things, got contacts and she did great. In fact, she promised me I would love them as well. "Oh, Mom, I can see so much better. No more glasses to hurt your nose and ears. And don't I look cooler? You should get some," she told me.

Katie had a good point. I remembered back to a pair of glasses I'd lost months earlier and subsequently replaced. Then this new pair fell onto my chair in a dark movie theater and I sat on them, bending the frame. Plus there was the constant nuisance of removing smudges. "Only use this special treated cloth or you'll scratch them," the optician warned me. I lost that cloth the first week.

I made an appointment with my eye doctor. I got contacts. It's true my life has not been the same since then—but then my life was never very normal compared to most people's in the first place.

Initially, the doctor wanted me to wear just one torque lens, he called it, to help correct my astigmatism. He explained the contact had a "weighted end" to it, so I needed to make sure the weight was at the bottom when I put it in. If I didn't, it would eventually move around all by itself. "Do what?" I said. Oooooooh, that made me nervous. Plus, wearing just one contact instead of two was not balanced—and I like balance. So I went back and he put in one torque lens and one regular lens. Oddly, one was tinted blue and was large. The other one was smaller and was clear. You guessed it. I went right back to the doctor and he tried two identical contacts for my two eyes.

Things went okay for a while, but then I experienced a dry, itchy feeling in both eyes. That's when I noticed little scratches on the contacts. The doctor said I would have to cut my fingernails. "Getting kind of personal, aren't we?" I asked with a raised eyebrow.

I did the manicure-thing and, sure enough, no more ripped contacts. Then spring came, and with it, allergies. Through red, watery sclerae, I stayed focused (no pun intended) and kept the little things firmly planted in my eyes.

Speaking of planting, I managed to get potting soil in my eyes one day when I dug a flower bed. This was the most painful experience yet, and it convinced me that glasses aren't so bad after all. When I got in the house I removed the contacts and threw them in the trash. The night of the dirt-in-the-eyes experience, I couldn't sleep I was so uncomfortable. After I finally did fall asleep, I woke up at 3 a.m. and put in eye drops.

I've concluded this about corrective eye wear: Contacts aren't for everyone. Oh sure, I wear them from time to time when I really want to see what's going on and when I'm too vain to do the four-eyes thing. But on any normal, given day, give me my glasses. After all, they are practically without problems.

Now, if I can just remember where I last laid them down…

The Lizard and the Rug

Few things make a woman jump faster and farther than creatures invading her home. The slimier, sneakier, and quicker they are, the worse they are.

I had my husband climb out our bedroom window one night when a cricket would not stop chirping. He stepped on the critter and the noise ceased. True, this was an exception to the rule, because the insect was in its own territory. But that's beside the point.

Every time my mother (who lives in North Carolina) comes to visit, deep into the night when we are having a serious mother-daughter talk, invariably there appears a huge, black South Carolina waterbug. Palmetto bugs, the locals call them. (I think Palmettos are the state bug.) To make matters worse, the nasty creature usually scurries across the kitchen counter. There go three days of cleaning down the tube.

Our conversation goes something like this. "Yes, Ann, you always were a weird child, so different from the rest of the family. And yes, Ann, we often wonder if you were adopted. The truth is—Oh my gosh! There's a six-inch, slimy, armed bug darting across your kitchen counter. Eeeek! Are you going to kill him?"

To which I say, "Either that, or put a leash around his neck and march him outside where he belongs."

But nothing could prepare me for the lizard. Naturally, it appeared one night when we had a friend over, one of my daughter's old college roommates. As we caught up on the latest news, someone (perhaps me) shrieked, "What was that?" as a long, green object streaked across the floor. We all jumped onto the couch. Not really, but we wanted to.

I assigned each available person to a post: our twenty-five-year-old daughter, Kelly, to the foyer; her friend the back door (guest or not, we were in this thing together now); our eleven-year-old daughter, Katie, the kitchen door; me, anywhere; and my six-foot-two, 200-pound, hunky husband Russell, everywhere.

It slid by us again. "Yikes! A lizard!" I screamed. It was no use. We couldn't locate him, much less catch him. There was only one thing to do at this point. Run upstairs to my bedroom and cry. But first I announced I would never (and I emphasized *never*) sleep in that house another night until my husband caught the lizard. Well, three months and ninety sleepless nights later, our eleven-year-old— not my big brave husband—did indeed locate the ill-fated reptile.

Here's how: One day I was sweeping the hardwood floors and vacuuming the area rug (the one my interior designer friend labeled "perfect"), when Katie yelled, "Mom, there he is!" "What are you talking about? Here who is?" I replied. She held back one corner of the rug to show me. I looked, and, indeed, there he was. Laid out flat, spread-eagled. He would have provided great incentive for a science project, but I decided we had unknowingly held onto him long enough, and off he went to lizard heaven.

As I said, few things make a woman jump faster and farther than creatures invading her home. Someone can yell, "Fire!" and I honestly don't think we'd panic any more than we do when we see a critter. Heart attacks, tornadoes, floods—nothing makes me move that fast. But when I hear, "Lizard," I'm outta there.

The Day the Alligator's Noose Got Loose

When I was about ten years old, we awoke one morning to a very unwelcome guest. Our two dogs, Spot and Lady, had barked and cried all night long. When Dad woke up at daybreak, he looked out the kitchen window and saw the dogs perched on top of their doghouse. They were still barking.

Dad walked outside to their pen and found an alligator. The creature was about three feet long and appeared trapped in the dog pen. All the neighborhood children heard the commotion and before long, one by one, they came to see the spectacle. This was big news for our little neighborhood.

Now, my dad loved to play jokes on people—harmless, he believed, but jokes all the same. He called a neighbor and they tied the alligator's mouth closed, my mother standing on its snout, shaking all over with fear. They put the creature in the trunk of our car, then drove the car to Dad's mechanic. Dad explained that his tire needed to be changed and the spare tire was in the trunk.

The mechanic, a very large macho-man, opened the trunk. My father and his friend watched from a distance. Though no one could have predicted the outcome (would the mechanic shout? run? faint?) everyone was in for a big shock, including my dad. The alligator had worked itself loose from the noose, and his mouth was wide open. No one got hurt, luckily, as the mechanic immediately shut the trunk. Actually, they all had a good laugh, the mechanic included.

Dad got a little more serious then and decided that perhaps the local high school biology teacher could use the reptilian specimen for the class to study. He would do a good deed by donating the alligator to science and be rid of the pest all at the same time. Dad was so proud of his brilliant idea. He got dressed in his best suit and drove over to the high school, whereupon Mr. Godwin, the teacher, politely informed my dad he was simply not interested. I believe he even went so far as to turn up his nose at the idea.

So Dad did what any good-hearted, confused alligator-catcher would do. He drove down to the swampy river and threw him back. But first he had a stern talk with the creature: "You're not wanted— not by dog, man, mechanic, or teacher. Go home." And we never saw the alligator again.

The Mayor and the Mustache

When I was younger and much more ambitious, I decided to go back to school. I was going to be a dental hygienist and get to look down people's throats all day. More importantly, I could do all the talking and no one would be able to stop me. I graduated from a two-year program and set sights on a job an hour away from the college.

I found the perfect position in a small seaside town and quickly fell in love with the patients. It seemed all was going well. One day I had the distinct pleasure of cleaning the teeth of one of the town's most prominent citizens—the mayor. Not just any mayor, but a tall, handsome, dark-haired gentleman with a thick mustache.

I made special preparations for his visit that day. I cleaned the entire dental unit until the chrome was blinding, Armor All'ed the leather chair, scrubbed the sink until it sparkled, and triple-sanitized the carpet.

We said our customary "how do you do's" and chatted just a few moments before I got down to serious work. With the dental mirror in one hand and curette in the other, I cleaned his teeth manually, as was the norm. I began with tooth #1. The mayor's fastidious care of his teeth made my work easy. That is, until tooth #23. Aha! Just enough calculus to force me to whip out my sickle scale—nicknamed Silver Pick—with its glistening, razor-sharp edge. With wrists rotating, elbows flying, the heel of my foot jammed into the carpet for support, I scraped and scraped, using more tactile sensitivity than sight.

"Ha!" I wanted to shriek. "No mercy! Once again, I reign victorious!" But I didn't utter a sound. With great self-control and dignity, I stood upright and surveyed the mayor. He was lying there as peacefully as if he were sunbathing. Things were going great, so I moved on to part two, polishing the mayor's now plaque-free teeth.

In my most professional voice, I offered him a choice of cherry, bubble gum, or mint-flavored polish for the next step. Then, gently placing the spinning rubber cup on his teeth and slowly engaging the floor pedal, I set to work covering his teeth with grit.

About the third tooth along his eyes began to water and his mouth began to twitch. Within seconds, one entire side of his face took on a twisted, pinched look. What the heck? I wondered. He raised his finger to point, and I saw that his hand and arm were shaking. An uncontrollable tremor had seized his entire body. His wide, frightened eyes pleaded for help.

Well! Of all things! His mustache was caught in the handpiece. All the whirring and grinding had proceeded to twist the mayor's mustache—now indistinguishable from his upper lip and nose—so tight he could not move. Neither could I. I froze for what seemed like an eternity. I prayed for an earthquake, a hurricane, an air raid. When none of these came to pass, I did what any other hygienist would do in this situation. I yelled for my boss, the dentist, to help.

He came charging into the room. I passed the mustache-eating equipment from my trembling hand to his steady one. With one finger he switched gears on the handpiece from forward to reverse, and the thick, black—now curly—mustache let go.

I never saw the mayor after that visit, or after that moment, for that matter. Soon afterwards, I packed up my dozen or so instruments in the same blue plastic tackle box each student was assigned in dental hygiene school and hid them under my bed, where they have remained ever since.

I've just de-celebrated the twentieth anniversary of that fateful day with the mayor and the mustache, and the end of my dental career. The good news—for patients—is: I no longer clean teeth. The bad news is, whenever I see a mustache, I break out in a cold sweat and stagger around chanting, "Reverse! Reverse! Reverse!"

Body Work for People, Not Cars

I really like having a remote for my car, but it's just so embarrassing when, instead of unlocking the door with the remote, I accidentally pop the trunk. Have you ever done that? My policy in this situation is to nonchalantly pick up something—anything—from my trunk and examine it like I know exactly what I am doing. Then, when no one is watching (or even if they are), I gingerly place the item back in the trunk, punch the other remote button to unlock the car, and drive off.

About two weeks ago on a clear-blue-sky Saturday, I popped the trunk lid by mistake. Then I walked back there to pretend I was looking for something…but nothing was there. This was because I had just cleaned out and vacuumed my car. What an ordeal. Darned if I didn't strain a muscle in my lower back. For you old-timers (and descriptive Southerners), I'll just say my back "went out."

Here's how it happened. I cleaned out my trunk, laid all the junk on the sidewalk, and noticed the vast amount of sand that remained (no wonder they have beach erosion here, the sand's all in my trunk). I realized I couldn't reach the back of the trunk with the high-suction pump that had nearly sucked up my accelerator pedal five minutes earlier. So, being the creative person that I am, I climbed into the trunk and kneeled down on all fours, wrestling the monster vacuum until the hose reached the deepest, darkest, furthest corners. There was only one problem: "Ohhhhhhhhhhhhhh, my back," I moaned to no one in particular.

That was really only the beginning. Chasing the pain all night, I alternately took Advil and then used the heating pad. The next morning I drove over to my chiropractor's office where I get body work (for me, not my car) and darned if the chiropractor didn't also have a pulled back. Needless to say, I couldn't get any assistance or relief that particular day. There we were, each trying to top the other's story of just how badly we had wrenched our backs.

This scenario reminds me that in life, there aren't always easy solutions. Sometimes you have to settle for the lesser of two evils. Case in point: you can either have a messy trunk or a bad back. Maybe I need to just relax my standards and forget about trying to keep my trunk spotless. Who sees it anyway? If, on the other hand, I can't let this obsession go, maybe I can bribe Katie into vacuuming periodically. Wait a minute. What am I thinking? This is the same daughter who hasn't yet washed or vacuumed the car she inherited over a year ago. She recently admitted she'd only vacuumed our house two or three times in six years. Katie vacuum my trunk? Yeah, like that's going to happen...

Where's Spartanburg, and Can You Get There from Here?

Russell is in the dog house *again*. No, it's worse than that; he's in the dog kennel. We spent twenty-four hours in Spartanburg recently, ten of which were wasted, driving around trying to figure out how we (make that Russell) got lost.

In his defense, the roads were a tad bit confusing. You'd be on I-26, and you could see I-85 right there in plain view, but you couldn't find an exit or a sign for the life of you.

This was our first trip to Spartanburg. Not to worry: Katie printed out the directions from the Internet and we set out about noon-time, heading to Converse College for her Governor's School Academy program, where she would study flute for two weeks.

As Katie has gotten older she has gradually taken over the job as co-navigator, riding in the front seat. She's five inches taller than me, so when I sit in the back seat, my vision is totally obstructed. I couldn't see what stretched ahead of us, but that was okay because we arrived at the motel without one wrong turn. But from there on out, omigosh!

We decided to go to dinner and invited our good friends Suzanne and Stefani, also from Pawleys Island, to come along. They were staying in the same motel, and it seemed like a great idea until Russell got behind the wheel. Since I'd been riding in the back seat for over five hours, I claimed the front seat on the drive over to the restaurant. We left the Hampton Inn parking lot, and nearly an hour later we drove back into the same parking lot—not after dinner, but before. We had called the restaurant before we left, and Russell had gotten directions over the phone. They were perfect except for one small detail. The man who gave us the directions began by saying, "Get on I-26," and we could not find I-26. I begged Russell to go inside the Hampton Inn and get a map. He did. That was a shock. He came back out and off we went. We made it to dinner without a hitch.

The next day we arrived at Converse College without getting lost, but I have to tell you, this time Katie was back in the front seat, navigating. There was a terrific program for parents and students that afternoon. Made me proud to be a South Carolinian. After the presentation, I introduced myself to the founder of the school, Dr. Virginia Uldrick. I exclaimed, "This is so exciting. I feel just like I am here." Ever gracious and charming, she smiled and said, "You know what, you *are* here." Y'all know what I meant though, right?

We said goodbye and were encouraged by the staff to leave quickly (someone must have told them about my family's looooong farewells). I knew I would miss having Katie at home, but actually, I was more worried about finding our home without Katie in the car to navigate.

My worries were justified. For starters, we lost our car. Russell blames that on me because he said I jumped out of the car and began walking so fast, he forgot to make a mental note of where he parked. Our goal was to meet Suzanne in the parking lot, as we were planning to follow her out of town. Luckily she pulled up about the time we realized we were lost and gave us a ride, driving around all three lots until we spotted our Buick.

At this point, Russell swore he knew the route and Suzanne actually believed him, falling in right behind us. Fifteen minutes later we were lost big-time—driving around a beautiful Spartanburg subdivision with stately colonials and mammoth brick mansions. The next thing I knew, we ended up in the Quincy's Restaurant parking lot, where the dinner crowd was beginning to congregate. I would have asked one of the guests where we were, but no, Russell insisted on going inside. He still won't admit it, but I think he stood in the dinner line for an hour before he ever spoke to anyone.

Despite the helpful new directions, guess where we ended up? In the same parking lot of the Hampton Inn in Spartanburg. I decided I was in a bad dream. That's when Russell started fussing, and I started feeling sorry for him. I patted him on the shoulder, saying,

"Well, honey, don't be so hard on yourself. You know we're our own worst enemies." He replied, "Yeah, but sometimes our spouses vie for that position." Who, me?

The rest of the trip only got worse. It took another hour to find a bathroom. When we finally did, it had a big sign that said, "Unisex." Whatcha gonna do? I went inside and nearly passed out from ammonia fumes, which were coming from a pail of water with a mop stuck in it. They were out of soap and paper towels and only had two squares of toilet paper. Here's what they also had: a fire extinguisher and a machine with personal products that I won't name. As we left the building, I recapped my bathroom experience for Russell, and he said, "What do you expect from a place that has bars on the windows?"

From there on out, we didn't make another wrong turn. Only one problem—we've lost the map and I think the jury is in: I'm bad luck in the front seat. We have to drive back up there in two weeks to get our navigator/daughter, and maybe we won't get lost coming home. I just hope we can *find* Spartanburg in the first place!

Big Hair Means the Big Time (Commitment, That Is)

Big hair is BIG in the South (and making a national return)! If you don't believe it, just sashay into the closest grocery store, or better yet, check out the local barbecue emporium. You'll see a herd of cashiers with big hair. It's a funny thing about women's hair. Like a lot of other matters in life, we never want what we have, and we often wish we had someone else's.

I woke up one dreary January morning, ready for a new me, a new life, or at least a new hairdo. That was it! A new do. I've always promised myself that one day—actually whenever I could get up the nerve—I would cut my hair real short and color it red. That particular morning I heard Mary Chapin Carpenter singing "I Feel Lucky" on the radio, which I took as a sign to get moving.

I drove straight to my hairdresser, and she cut my hair real short ("up over my ears," as she called it). I loved it. My next mission was to go to the local beauty supply, where you can buy hair products just like the ones the professionals use, but without the high cost. The only catch is, the store's staff can't give advice. So if you pick up a bottle of hair color and ask, "Will this turn my hair green?" they can't tell you, and they'll tell you they can't tell you. "Only if you're a licensed hairdresser can we give advice," they say, with a smirk. "Oh, and you have to have a card to prove you're one. That's the state law."

I bought a bottle of copper-colored hair dye with a generic label. It looked innocent enough. I came home, followed the directions on the bottle, and screamed when I saw that my brunette hair was now dark burgundy. It was late at night and the beauty shops were closed, so I called a hairdresser friend who told me to use Dawn dishwashing detergent. I told her this had nothing to do with my dishes, but she insisted. It would lighten up my hair a shade or two, she said. It did. Now my hair was medium burgundy instead of dark burgundy.

146

For the next ten months, I did lots of experimenting with color, cut, and style. My current favorite hairdo is big hair. I have a neighbor who has gorgeous big hair, and I inquired one day as to how she styled her coif. She just blushed (she is so darn sweet) and said "Gosh, honey, I don't know. I just wash it and fix it and it comes out like this." Right. I decided to try some investigating on my own.

You see, mornings are always rough on me and my hair. When I wake up, invariably my hair is sticking straight out. I look in the mirror and feel like McCaulay Culkin when he slapped his face in "Home Alone." I can't leave the house looking like that. After some experimenting, I finally figured out the secret of big hair and here it is: I jump in the tub quick before anyone can see me. I wash and rinse my hair, jump out of the tub, and towel it dry. Then I get creative. I lather in about two ounces of mousse—the strong stuff. I begin blow-drying these medium-burgundy (thanks to Dawn) tendrils. I lean over, and all the blood rushes to my face. No one said it would be easy. I rub hard, hard, hard, until my scalp is aching, all the while still blow-drying. I shake my head in all directions. I spray hairspray (extra-hold, of course). I continue to blow-dry. When my hair is almost dry (this step is very important) I use three fingers at the part in front and push, push, push to get some height. I apply more mousse. I apply more hairspray. I look in the mirror. Yes! That's it! I take out the hairspray one final time, lacquer down the whole mess, and dare it to move. Perfect. Big hair!

One day it hits me. All those grueling steps, when an hour earlier that's basically how my hair looked as I rolled out of bed. Well, maybe that's not entirely true. It's not as shiny or kempt, and though it does have height, it has no volume. I give up. Now I'm back to washing, conditioning, moussing, blow-drying, and finger-styling.

The ultimate compliment came the other day when a lady asked me, "How do you get your hair to stand up like that?" "Sorry," I answered, "I can't give advice unless you are a licensed, card-carrying hairdresser—that's the law."

Some Folks Lose Things, Some Get Lost

I wonder if it is a sign of old age when we start losing things. I'd prefer to think in my case it is because of my high IQ (can't handle the small, mundane things), but some people, whom I refuse to name, would disagree.

The strangest incident happened the day I lost my daughter, who was six at the time. Or should I say she lost me? After school and the usual carpooling, I ran back to church to pick her up from choir. The minister and I drove up to the parking lot at the same time. He walked over to my car and asked how I was doing.

"Fine," I said, smiling. "I'm here to pick up Katie from choir."

He asked, "Katie? I believe the three-year-olds' choir is practicing today. Isn't Katie about six?"

I thought for a moment, then gasped. "Oh my gosh, you're right! She's at dance lessons." I made the minister promise not to ever tell anyone this happened. Never mind the fact that I am now telling anyone who'll listen.

A few years later I lost my car. It was during Katie's eleventh birthday party. Russell and I drove separate cars, each one full of gangly, giggly girls, to see "The Indian in the Cupboard." When the movie was over, we said goodbye and walked to our respective cars. We planned to meet back at our house for ice cream and cake. Russell was long gone by the time we'd trudged through the huge mall parking lot in the ninety-degree July heat. The car was nowhere to be found. Our parade prompted more than a few curious onlookers, and many people stopped to help. Almost an hour later we walked back into the mall, retraced our steps, and realized there were two entrances—front and back. I'll let you figure out what I did wrong.

My sister Cathy, who lived in Italy for three years, came to visit me recently after moving back to Virginia. She begged me to take her shopping, and off we went to Lowe's. I should tell you that she says shopping in Italy is altogether different from shopping in America. I've never seen anyone get so excited over carpet, tile, and tools. As I walked to the register to pay, Cathy reassured me she was right behind me.

Well, I turned around—and, just that quick, she was gone. I had lost my grown sister in the Lowe's Superstore. I did what any concerned, worried mother has been trained to do when she loses a child. I went to the information desk and had her paged. Moments later she came running up with a cart full of stuff. The small crowd that had gathered stared in shock as Cathy came forward. I guess they expected to see a child. I found myself standing there, scolding her, saying I had worried that she was lost. Cathy corrected me, saying in a childlike voice that she did not get lost. "Really," she said, "I just got side-tracked."

I'm glad I found my sister, but sad that I lost my sapphire-and-diamond ring I'd bought in the Bahamas. Our family went on a cruise last year, and I purchased a new ring. In all the excitement of leaving the ship, I dropped it into my purse. Now it's gone, and I'm still searching for it. I just know it will show up one day. It's probably in that same mysterious place I lost my keys, my glasses, and my common sense. Hold on, I'm going to look right now.

chapter 6

Granny Pinky:
The Grande Dame

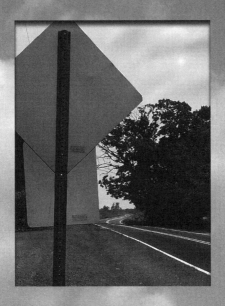

Pay-Ya Preserves and Fickled Pigs

Granny Pinky had the strongest Southern accent of any North Carolinian I ever knew. She had a few words we loved to tease her about, and one of them was *pear*. To her, it was *pay-ya*.

She had an old pear tree growing in her yard. It yielded huge, dull-green fruit with brown specks. These pears were so hard you could almost break a tooth, but were good for canning.

Granny had a young neighbor named David, about nine years old, who worked for her from time to time. He would mow the lawn on days her arthritis was acting up, bring in her newspaper, or do any other odd job she had. Looking back, I think he was more company to her than anything else, though she'd never admit it.

Once when she was "putting up pay-yas," as she would say, she offered David a jar as he was finishing a job and getting ready to go home. "David, would you like some pay-ya preserves?" she asked.

David replied, "Thank you, Miss Pinky. I'll let you know." He took the jar from her and left. She wrinkled her forehead, confused, but shuffled back into the living room to finish watching an episode of "The Young and the Restless."

A few minutes later, she heard a knock at the door. David stood there smiling. "Miss Pinky, you didn't say how much to pay ya for the pay-ya preserves, but I figured seventy-five cents would be about enough. Then I tasted them on a cold biscuit, and I decided they're worth every bit a dollar or more." He pushed the wadded-up dollar bill into the palm of her hand and ran off.

David wasn't the only one who enjoyed her preserves. So did

her granddaughters—so much so that we urged Granny to teach us how to can, and she did. After we got good at it, we shared our bounty with friends and family. One time my sister and I were putting up figs. They grow so large and sweet in the South, and we Southerners find ways to use figs you could not imagine. Jelly, preserves, cakes—you name it, we've done it. Granny came in late one afternoon to eat dinner with us. She asked Cathy, my oldest sister, what she was cooking at the stove. "Here, try one," Cathy said. "I'm putting up some fickled pigs."

To this day, we serve pickled figs and pear preserves at Christmas, and any other special time we choose. We even have a designated crystal dish with divided compartments for these two goodies. But we always ask before we pass the plate, "Would you like some pay-ya preserves, or do you prefer fickled pigs?"

Rat Cheese and Common Courtesy

When we lived at Bear Creek, North Carolina, the local-yokel grocery store was called the Red Barn. It was down a winding two-lane road that turned into gravel at the end. The shop sat right on the edge of the creek. Appropriately named, the red, barn-shaped building sold fishing supplies, ice cream, bottled Cokes in a red cooler, and rat (or hoop) cheese that sat in a box, the red rind encasing the huge orange wheel.

Now, Granny Pinky would go to the Red Barn every few days, and she always bought the rat cheese that had just a little mold on it, because they gave her a discount. ("No one will ever notice," she would say.)

The owner or his wife would cut her a huge hunk, and that was what she said was the secret ingredient to her meatless spaghetti. She wouldn't make the spaghetti without her special cheese, and I don't know if she'd make it without the store-bought mold, which she swore she removed first.

Granny would sometimes call ahead to make sure an item was available before driving over. She had a bad habit of not identifying herself on the telephone. When the person answered, she would just go directly into whatever was on her mind. Also, she never said goodbye when she hung up. Our family got used to it, knowing it was her because of what she *didn't* say.

Once she called the Red Barn and simply asked, "You got any rat cheese—." The person on the other end interrupted, "No, but we got a mouse in the trap last night," at which point Granny gasped and hung up.

Granny turned to me and ranted, "Well, I have never! He didn't even let me finish. I wanted to know if he had any rat cheese—with mold." Not taking no for an answer, she immediately drove down to the Red Barn and bought a pound of her special cheese. A new employee, a pimply teenage boy, waited on her. He turned ten shades of red when she told him she was the one who had just telephoned.

Granny had lots of other uses for rat cheese: open-faced toasted (nearly burnt) cheese and tomato sandwiches, pimento cheese, and macaroni and cheese. For this last dish, she would make a sauce of butter, flour, eggs, and black pepper. She said this "thickened the concoction." She added the sauce to the cooked, drained noodles, then put in hunks of cheese, saving some grated pieces for the top. The final step was baking the dish in a hot oven, which was never hot enough to suit her. When no one was watching, she'd turn on the broiler. Oftentimes, with Granny not paying attention to the oven, the casserole's golden-brown top would get blackened beyond recognition. It got to where whenever our family was invited to dinner, we'd arrive an hour early so one of us could be assigned to "burn control." You can see why somebody had to keep an eye on her!

Granny Pinky and the Shoe Stretcher

Granny Pinky was probably the best salesclerk Dad ever had. She was part hostess/comedian/hospitality chairperson and part fashion expert. She would arrive at The Bootery, our family shoe store, dressed to the nines with her red lipstick, matching fingernails, and short, perfectly combed salt-and-pepper hair. Granny was tall—about five-foot-nine—and stout. She had a heart-shaped face with small dark blue eyes that disappeared when she laughed and tiny, perfect rosebud lips. She also had a prominent nose and was the first to make fun of herself, claiming she had a Roman nose: "It roams all over my face."

Truth be told, I think a lot of customers came in just to see her. Many times her opinion weighed so heavily with our local clientele that it would actually make or break a sale.

When a woman stuffed her size-ten foot into an eight-and-a-half shoe, Granny would be honest: "Phew, if you buy those shoes, your feet are going to kill you. I'm telling you now, that looks mighty tight to me." Always eager to solve a problem, she'd offer to help. "Here, let me stretch that pa-ya (pair) for you real quick-like." Then she'd disappear into the back room and stretch the shoe (though it didn't look any larger afterwards), so the customer would be more comfortable.

Once I walked in when Granny was stretching a pair of high heels. She picked up the stretching contraption, stuffed it into the toe of the shoe, and began to turn the knob so that the wooden triangle could expand the leather. She was talking to me and turning the knob when we heard a strained sound. It was the leather stretching, nearly separating the sole from the shoe. Granny looked down, unscrewed the stretcher, and firmly squeezed the shoe with her thumb and forefinger. She turned toward me and asked, "It's all right, don't you think? No one will ever notice."

We never worked on commission, but from time to time, Dad would run "P.M. Specials." P.M. stood for prize money, but it could have stood for Pinky Morris, since she usually sold the most. We would get fifty cents per sale of a particular item as our reward, and the money quickly added up. Dad would announce on Monday that we were running a special on pocketbooks, for instance, and by Friday they'd be nearly gone. On the big day the sale was to begin, we would get there an hour and a half before opening just to see the customers line up outside the building. It reminded me of a movie line, and why not? The bargains were terrific, and our store was the place to be and be seen.

It wasn't unusual for customers to drive from as far as New Bern, Kinston, or Wilmington. Some came from sixty miles away. Word of the sales spread quickly, and people made a day of it. Neighbors would get reacquainted during the frenzy and you could hear them catching up on all the latest gossip. On those days, Granny usually greeted the customers, then walked around the store, chatting. Once they'd made their purchases and were loaded down with packages, she would see them off. Opening the door, she'd smile and wave like Andy Griffith, saying, "Y'all come back, y'hear?" And they almost always did!

Red Bows and Painted Toes

Granny Pinky had only one pet that I ever knew about, and his name was Marquis LeBlanc Morris. He was a white French poodle and her baby. Of course, she would never admit that. She called him Mark for short, and they were inseparable.

She would often take Mark to get his hair and nails done, as she called it. He would return home with a red bow in his hair and red nails. "Nothing pink for this boy," she'd say. "I don't want him looking like a sissy!" On those days, and those days alone, she'd fuss over him. She talked baby talk and would give him doggie biscuits when he returned home. Any other time, it was business as usual.

Whenever Granny left her house, Mark would get on a chair and part the curtains with his nose, watching and waiting all day for her to come home. Then she'd come barreling through the door and fuss, "Wasn't gone that long. What mischief did you get into?"

On the weeks he didn't go to the Downtown Doggie Salon, Granny bathed him herself. She had a specific ratty, stained beach towel she used just for Mark's bath. The problem was, as soon as he saw her pick up the towel, he took off running and hid under the bed. No coaxing or bribing would get him to budge.

Now Mark had a habit, as many dogs do, of barking ferociously when the doorbell rang. He could have been a great watchdog, but the truth is, he wouldn't hurt a flea. And I'm sure he never had one on his pampered, powdered body.

Finally, Granny figured out what to do. She would sneak into the linen closet, grab that special towel, and lay it out beside the tub. Next, she tiptoed out the back door, ran around to the front porch, and rang the doorbell. Mark would come running and barking, ready to "protect" his master. Before he knew what was happening, Granny would run into the house, swoop him up, and throw him in the tub.

In all those years, he never caught on and she never had to pull him out from under the bed again.

Granny Pinky's Stolen Plymouth and the Fourth of July

When my parents moved to Bear Creek, the Fourth of July became the family's all-time favorite holiday. We invited all our relatives, neighbors, and friends and had a cookout complete with homemade ice cream. Dad would drive to Myrtle Beach a week beforehand to buy the fireworks—a yearly ritual in itself.

Granny Pinky lived only seven-tenths of a mile away, but she always drove down on the Fourth because it would be dark when she left. One year when the party broke up, she told us goodbye but within minutes burst back into the house.

"Someone stole my car," she hollered.

"Mother, now, surely you're mistaken," Dad said, puzzled.

He walked out the back door with her and, sure enough, her car was gone.

Dad asked her to point to where she last saw it, and Granny nearly hit him with her pocketbook. They walked down the road and came back. It was dark, but the moon was bright, and she and Dad came home disgusted. Sure enough, someone had stolen her car.

We all sat there dumbfounded at the kitchen table, with Dad looking up the sheriff's number, when up drove eighty-five-year-old Mr. Atlas going about ninety miles an hour. It seemed Mr. Atlas had a car just like Granny's, and with his bad memory and all, he just forgot he hadn't driven that night. At least that's what we surmised later.

He came into the house and spoke slowly and deliberately. "Miss Pinky, you should never, ever leave your keys in your car. Didn't you know someone could steal it?" Without saying a word, Granny took the keys and followed him down the stairs and out the door.

We watched from the window as Granny fussed at him. "Atlas,

you nearly drove my car into the ri-va [river], going so fast!" They both climbed in and she sped away to Mr. Atlas's house, which, by the way, was only two doors down from her own.

Before the day of the lost car, Granny parked wherever she landed, never paying much attention. After that incident, though, she parked her car as close to her house as possible. She had a concrete driveway that ended beside a screened-in back porch. Granny would pull up and leave just enough room between the automobile and the wall to get herself out. She also began keeping her keys in one particular kitchen drawer. I suspect she checked a couple of times per day to make sure her Plymouth was sitting there.

Granny was also famous for another car episode. She once drove up to the local grocery and parked in the fire lane. I'm sure she saw the sign, but she must have been in her usual hurry and ignored it. She ran in to get three or four items, then drove on home. About an hour later, my dad called and fussed at her for parking illegally. She wanted to know how he knew and he almost didn't tell her. At her insistence, he finally gave in. It seems a local police officer (and a good friend of my dad's) called him at home. He had recognized the Plymouth and knew it belonged to my dad's mother. But hey, at least the cop didn't have the vehicle towed away. Then Granny would have thought her car was stolen once again!

The Never-Ending Afghan

Granny Pinky loved to crochet—maybe because it produced quick results, or because she could do it while watching John Wayne reruns or her daily soap operas. But as was the case with many of the other things she did, she never followed directions. Be it a crocheting or sewing pattern, a recipe, or directions out of town, she usually "winged it" and surprised us by usually, though not always, coming out okay in the end. I remember the day she showed me the shapeless afghan.

It turned out she was making a granny-square afghan when she became engrossed in a TV show. The crochet needles were flying in her nimble hands just inches above the ball of yarn in her lap. The speed, coupled with "All My Children," caused her to lose her concentration, so she didn't notice that the rows of stitches were uneven, and becoming more so with each stitch. It was more like they were totally lopsided. As she tried in vain to make her final stitch, she discovered she couldn't. In fact, the original four corners were gone. Only an odd, woolly shape remained. She later said "that was the afghan that never ended."

Granny also tried sewing occasionally, but she didn't have too much luck with that either. She'd been known to stick herself with a needle a time or two, and when cutting out material, she once cut through the tablecloth underneath. While sewing, she often had trouble with the darts. She visited my mother once, wearing a sleeveless blouse she had made that hung an inch lower on one side than the other. "Pinky, what's wrong with that blouse?" my mother asked.

"Wrong? Nothing's wrong. I sewed this blouse myself, and the only problem that I can see—and it's minor—is the darts." One dart pointed up to her breast, and the other one pointed down to her waist.

My mother replied, "If you've got a minute, I'll be glad to fix that."

Granny marched right into the kitchen, poured herself a cup of coffee, and said, "Nah, no one will ever notice."

A Hot Stove and a Fast Car

We often joked that Granny Pinky's stove only had two settings: off and high. It was not uncommon to find her standing at the stove after the meal was cooked, scraping charred chicken or pulling the top off the cornbread. "No one will ever notice," she would tell me with a wink.

Her specialty was scorched fatback. She would cook it with a little bit of Crisco in a small black iron skillet, and before long the unmistakable smell of cooking fat permeated the whole house. She might go and open a kitchen window to "let it air out." Or she might pretend she didn't notice that the neighbors were only seconds away from calling the fire department.

In later years Granny ate a lot of sandwiches. I guess that was because they were "safe." Come to think of it, though, she did like to put them in her small toaster-oven that had two settings: broil and bake. (Selecting "bake" to cook the sandwich was the slower method, but yielded the perfect flavor.) She invented a lunch treat that she became famous for, at least in our family. She would lay a slice of cheese on a piece of white bread and top that with a couple of thick slices of homegrown tomato. Then she would sprinkle lots of salt and pepper. She loved adding pepper to nearly all dishes. Granny's open-faced sandwich was delicious—that is, if the cheese didn't puff up and turn black (meaning she'd broiled instead of baked it).

Granny's car was similar to her stove in that it had two speeds: fast and park. She bragged about her driving skills, and she drove herself all over North Carolina. Up until her very last days, at age eighty-something, she would pop in the car and go to the Pak-a-Sak, visit her daughter or two sons in Jacksonville, and maybe even go see her friend Shug in New Bern. These trips were usually spontaneous. She thrived on spur-of-the-moment excursions.

She also enjoyed riding around, stopping to look at new houses that were being built. Near her home in Bear Creek, there weren't any subdivisions. Instead, a single home would pop up now and then and we'd walk through the structure after the workmen had gone home. She always had an opinion and would tell me how she would have "done it differently" had it been her home. "Bathroom needs a window," she'd say. Or, "That kitchen is too small." When she'd finished adding her two cents' worth, she'd turn to leave without warning. If I was smart I'd already be close to the car because she'd zip off in a hurry, maybe not noticing if I was inside.

One day she was running late, and even though she didn't need an excuse she was speeding along in her green Plymouth when she heard a siren and saw a blue light behind her. She pulled over and when the officer approached her, he asked her, "Ma'am, didn't you see that yellow light?"

"See it? Of course I did. Why do you think I gunned it? I was trying to get through before the danged thing turned red."

He tipped his hat and walked back to his car, not writing her a citation—perhaps because she had a good point. Actually, I don't think she ever got a speeding ticket. I doubt she would have stayed still long enough for one to be written.

A Rich Inheritance, Indeed

From time to time as Granny Pinky got older, she had such aches and pains from her arthritis that she would proceed to call the doctor and get referred to another doctor, who referred her to another, and so forth and so on. She seemed to particularly enjoy the office visits out of town. Maybe it was because she enjoyed driving her fast Plymouth.

One time when she came home from such a visit, after describing every minute pain in detail she announced to the family that she didn't think she had much longer to live and she was ready to "divide up her things." At times like this my dad, aunt, and uncle would just let her give her little spiel and get it all out of her system. Then she would be fine for, oh, another ten years or so.

On one particular visit she was so sure her time was near that she came home and marked just about every piece of furniture, collectible, and memento as to who would get what when she "departed." She pulled out her masking tape and her laundry marker and proceeded to catalog the whole house.

One aunt got this and one niece got that and before long, her house was filled with names. She asked me what I wanted, and I told her quite simply and quite truthfully for her to get well.

When she did finally meet her maker, I was moved to receive a beautiful pink McCoy pitcher, a statue of an old man and woman, and three arborvitaes, which she'd had my husband dig up and plant in my own yard only months before. Mostly, though, she left me a legacy of love, not spoken often but shown—and enough stories to last me and my children a lifetime.

Acknowledgements

A debt of gratitude for my terrific family. They have supported me one-hundred percent and then some: Cathy Smith, Nancy Huxley, Steve and Lori Morris, and for my beautiful granddaughter, Madison, and my son-in-law, Chuck Stunda.

For dear friends who either appear in my stories or have given me great ideas for them: Pam Bell, Susie Collins, Terri Cox, Debbie Elmendorf, Beth Ervin, Madelene Fulcher, Carolyn Gee, Jean Hussey, Charlotte Kennerly, Sharon Mascow, Virginia Rowland, Jane Sawyer, Belinda Waslien, Regina Wells, and my supper club.

A special thanks to my editors, Emily Colin and Emily-Sarah Lineback, and thanks to Scott Whitaker of Whitline Ink for the superior book and cover design. You are the very best!

Thank you to all the people who gave me the platform to write and/or read my stories: Delores Blount, Susan Bryant, Ann Carlson, Linda Ketron, Jesse Tullos, Tom Warner and Vickie Crafton, and Beth Williams. For my writer friends, I am humbled and honored for your support: Dorothea Benton "Dottie" Frank, William P. "Billy" Baldwin, Beth Polson, and Nancy Rhyne.

A word of praise to Elizabeth Robertson Huntsinger whose expert opinion and advice are especially appreciated. We may be the tiniest writers group in the world, but we're also the most productive!

And a special note of appreciation to Rev. Ken Timmerman and Rev. Milton McGuirt, whose prayers have truly encouraged me and allowed my faith to grow.

And finally, to all the kindred spirits who said, "You can do it!": *Georgetown Times, Pee Dee Magazine*, Strand Media, *Sasee*, and *Gateway*. Also, First United Methodist Church in Myrtle Beach, St. Paul's Waccamaw United Methodist Church in Pawleys Island, Waccamaw Library, Georgetown Library and Chapin Library.